To

Enjoy the Faribault history!

FARIBAULT WOOLEN MILL

LOOMED IN THE LAND OF LAKES

[signature]

12.15

LISA M. BOLT SIMONS

Photography by Jillian Raye

THE
History
PRESS

Published by The History Press
Charleston, SC
www.historypress.net

To my husband, Dave; twins, Jeri and Anthony; dad (RIP), mom, brothers, nieces, nephews, cousins, in-laws and extended family; and to every single friend of mine. Life would not be the same without all of you.

CONTENTS

PREFACE

You're driving on I-35, just a mile or two from the first exit for Faribault, forty-five minutes south of Minneapolis, give or take rush hour. A billboard shows a woman's hands buckling a small belt around a folded wool blanket. The advertisement invites you to the factory store, exit 59. You've heard the name before, the Faribault Woolen Mill Company, and you decide to take a look.

You take the exit for Highway 21, cross back under the interstate and head south. You pass the locally owned Reliance Bank on your right, a new Super America on your left. At the second light, you turn left and drive past GrandStay and then Oma Pond with several wooden duck stands near and on the weedy, cat-tailed shore. Bethel Ridge Church is the pond's newer next-door neighbor to the north. Take a right at the three-way intersection after you pass the Rice County Fairgrounds. After several houses, you pass the Rice County Historical Society with its one-room schoolhouse and settlers' cabin. To the left is an office complex for Faribault Foods, which used to be the retail store for the Faribault Mills. Before you cross a bridge, you see the deep-sepia expanse of Cannon River Reservoir next to Alexander Park. The first dam spills onto mossy rock; a narrow pedestrian bridge crosses its width. The next dam, the Cannon River dam, sits next to a massive building: the Faribault Woolen Mill. Its main rectangular shape rises a few stories tall with time-worn white mortar between reddish bricks. A one-story rectangle extends to the left, newer brick on its face. Behind that, just as tall as the older building, is another multi-story rectangle covered in reddish-colored siding. A pistachio-green blower perches on one of the roofs. A brick chimney column juts into the sky, a reminder that this business still stands tall after 150 years.

Audrey Kletscher Helbling, who lives in Faribault, visited the store a month after its opening. On her Minnesota Prairie Roots blog, she wrote:

> *Rustic. Simplistic. Minimalist. Those words wash over me as I step into the Faribault Woolen Mill Company's recently reopened retail store. I could have strolled into an art gallery for the artsy vibe of this place. It has that feel, that sense of style and creative energy, which tells you this is no cookie-cutter retail outlet but someplace special.*

Rich brown barn wood lies wide on the wall behind the register. Forever in this wood, carved in cursive, is the name of forty-year employee Jas [James] H. Lockwood, with looping *os* and the tail of the *d* swirling up and then back under the name, forming a grin, the date 5-21-31 above the curved line. Off-white wainscoting, squared dark metal posts, sliding barn doors on metal rails and exposed ceiling beams all complement the remodeled space.

Blankets are everywhere. They drape metal pipes on the wall and lie perfectly folded on wooden shelves—blankets of solid colors, blankets with stripes, with fringe, even with maps of Minneapolis, St. Paul, New York and Brooklyn weaved into the fabric. A table showcases products for University of Minnesota fans. Old sewing machines give the place a sense of the mill's history, one that lends itself to a local-bred company that is now internationally known and cherished.

This book is not about just any woolen mill. It's about beginnings, change, success. It's about fire, failure, closing. It's about second, third and even fourth chances. It's about family. It's about Faribault.

The Faribault Woolen Mill Company.

ACKNOWLEDGEMENTS

First and foremost, though writing about the Faribault Woolen Mill had been a secret interest of mine, I would not have made the connection with The History Press if it weren't for Audrey Kletscher Helbling. Thank you for asking about my interest in the initial project.

To Greg Dumais, Hilary Parrish, Anna Burrous and everyone else at The History Press—thank you for everything.

I also want to extend my utmost appreciation to the people at the Faribault Woolen Mill: Paul, Jean, Bruce, Jana, Dennis, Dana, Mary, Sammy, Avinash, Vishal, Mikayla, "Anna," Tom, Terry, John, Jake, Joe and all the rest, past and present. Your histories, time and stories are truly a gift. Thank you, as well, to Tom and Pete for sharing your family stories. I also need to thank my former co-worker turned awesome photographer, Jillian, for her friendship and keen eye. Also, thank you to Jeff and LaVonne's *Book of Memories*. Thank you to Sue and Libby at the Rice County Historical Society–Faribault and Mee and Anne at the Southern Minnesota Historical Center at Minnesota State University–Mankato. To Holly, thank you for your expertise; you saved me time and stress. Tim and Jenny, thank you for a place to get away from real-life distractions to work. Thank you to Lisa Red, Joleen, Mary Beth, Nancy, Betty and Claire for the pep talk, encouragement and cheek-aching laughter. Thank you to Mark at Apple, who saved my sanity. Thank you to everyone who listened and cheered: Amber, Emily, Kuresha, Lauren, Molly, Nichole, Robin, Sara, Tara and the rest at Roosevelt; Brandi, Gloria, Kristi and Rachael; and my 4B and Bunko groups.

ACKNOWLEDGEMENTS

A fond nod of gratitude to Yvonne, Patti, Georgia and Traci in Shabooks, as well as Phyllis, Pearl and Dorothy in my Faribault Writers' Club. Thanks to the Northfield writing group—Donna, Sharon and Torild—for your enthusiasm when I shared.

A book is most definitely a team effort, and I'm so sorry if I forgot anyone's name.

Finally, I did my best to synthesize the mill's vibrant historical information and provide interesting images in less than a year, though this is truly a years-long worthy project.

Note: For extracted quotations, I took the liberty of correcting some minor errors, such as a capital versus a lowercase letter, that did not affect the meaning of the text.

CHAPTER 1

CARL KLEMER AND THE
ONE-HORSE MILL

On January 20, 1824, a boy named Carl Henry Klemer was born near Berlin, Germany. Not much is known about his parents or siblings; no diary or journal has been found. What is known is that Carl moved to America, most likely alone. He made his way to Watertown, Wisconsin, when he was twenty-four years old.

His trade was cabinetmaking.

In Chicago, sometime in the mid-1800s, he married Fredricka Steffens. It's unknown if they met in the United States or if Fredricka traveled from Germany to join him once he settled. With immersion and learning what he needed, Carl picked up the English language and settled in with his new wife.

In 1854, still in Watertown, Carl and Fredricka welcomed their son Henry. In 1856, son Ferdinand was born. The next year, Carl packed his young family's belongings in a wagon and moved them by oxen to a farm near Nerstrand, Minnesota.

Seven years later, Carl sold his farm and moved to Faribault. There, Jacob Wandell hired Carl, who worked once again as a cabinetmaker.

Family tales and local lore swirl around the real reason Carl decided to buy his first carding machine. Perhaps he discussed the proposition with his wife. Perhaps he read about the mill in Minneapolis, the future North Star Woolen Mill, and mentioned nothing to his wife. Carl's grandson Frank Klemer wrote the "History of Faribault Woolen Mills: 1865–1940," which he presented to the Rice County Historical Society in October 1940. Frank was told by his dad, Henry, "that it was an old English carder who made

Son Ferdinand Klemer, Carl Klemer and son Henry Klemer: the first two generations of the mill. *Photo by author, Faribault Woolen Mill Archives.*

the suggestion to Mr. Klemer that he buy a card and start carding wool for growers." Another theory centers on an editorial in the *Faribault Republican* that claimed the town needed a carder to keep up with all the sheep. No matter the reason, Carl bought his carding machine on May 24, 1865. Though not yet the Faribault Woolen Mill Company, thus begins its story.

FARIBAULT

The town that became the home of the woolen mill was named for one of its first full-time residents, Alexander Faribault, pronounced "Fair-uh-bow." Alexander, born in 1806 to a French Canadian fur trader and a woman from the Dakota tribe, moved to Minnesota from Wisconsin around 1819. He built his first trading post next to the Cannon River at the age of twenty. Eight years later, he moved the trading post to the intersection of the Cannon River and Straight River. The town of Faribault eventually grew south of this river intersection.

Alexander wasn't the only settler who invested in the area. L.E. Swanberg, a former *Faribault Daily News* reporter and editor, edited the 1976 book *Then*

& Now: A History of Rice County, Faribault & Communities. In it, other settlers are mentioned, including Peter Bush, Luke Hulett, Edward LeMay, Narcisse Arpan, Henry Millard, Joseph Dashner, E.J. Crump, Reverend Standish and John Geckler. In the winter of 1853, seventeen family names were listed as residents. "According to available records," the book stated, "Alexander Faribault, Peter Bush and Luke Hulett should be considered the founders of the first settlement in Rice County." When the town was platted on February 17, 1855, Alexander, F.B. Sibley, John W. North and Porter Nutter filed. Why Faribault was chosen as the name rather than Hulett or Bush can only be speculated. North established Northfield, about fourteen miles northeast of the town of Faribault; John Morris established Morristown, about twelve miles southwest.

Minnesota became a territory in 1849 and a state nine years later. During this time, Alexander built the first wood-frame house, which still stands, renovated by the Rice County Historical Society; the first school was built; and mail service started. In the spring of 1856, the town had 20 buildings. By fall, that number had grown to 250.

The same year Minnesota became a state, Henry Whipple became the first Episcopal bishop, and Shattuck School, now called Shattuck–St. Mary's, was founded. In November and December 1862, as the United States battled in the Civil War, the Dakota War began because of land treaty conflicts with the government. For six weeks some Dakota warriors fought white settlers, while other Dakota people protected the settlers. In Mankato, about forty-five miles west of Faribault, 303 Dakota were imprisoned. On December 26, 1862, 38 Dakotas were hanged; it is still considered the largest mass execution in the history of the United States. While most of the Dakota fled Minnesota, both Alexander and Bishop Whipple provided support to the families who chose to settle in the town the next year.

The year 1863 saw the founding of the Minnesota State Academy for the Deaf, then called the Minnesota State Institute for the Education of the Deaf and Dumb. The next year, the name was changed to Minnesota Institute for the Deaf, Dumb and Blind. The school for students who were blind opened its own campus eleven years later.

In 1865, the first railroad line reached the town of Faribault. The following comes from the National Park Service registration form for the National Register of Historic Places for the Faribault Woolen Mill:

> *An extensive rail network served the community beginning in 1865 when a line of the Minnesota Railway Company (later the Chicago, Milwaukee, and Saint Paul) reached Faribault. The Chicago and Great Western*

Railway entered the city in 1882 and the Burlington, Cedar Rapids, and Northern (later the Chicago, Rock Island, and Pacific) followed in 1901. The Chicago and Great Western Railway entered the city in 1882 and the Burlington, Cedar Rapids and Northern (later the Chicago, Rock Island, and Pacific) followed in 1901. The city's size and diverse population supported both freight and passenger services from all three lines. The Chicago and Great Western line ran southeast of the Faribault Woolen Mill Company, which had become the main textile business in the city.

Also in 1865, the Catholic school Bethlehem Academy opened its doors to eighteen students and Carl Klemer bought his first carding machine.

A ONE-HORSE MILL

In June 1865, after Carl advertised his new business in the *Faribault Republican*, he started carding wool in a building on Fourth Street and Second Avenue Northwest. A horse named Jenny, according to a Klemer relative, walked on a treadmill to lend the power. The other piece of equipment Carl had was a picker. This tore apart the wool in order to ready it for the carding process.

To visualize carding, imagine children's bushy heads of morning hair on a camping trip and brushes held by several adults. Carding combs through raw wool and blends it. It also combs it to lie in the same direction. Klemer's carding those first couple of years combed the wool into batting, a sort of fluffy sheet that women took home and used for quilts or spun into yarn.

On March 13, 1867, the *Faribault Republican* published a report on the mill business. Klemer had replaced the power of Jenny with a different horse power: a five-horsepower steam engine. The steam engine had been invented more than a century earlier and now provided Klemer with five times the power of his one horse. This new machine produced about twelve thousand pounds of carded wool in one year. The business was referred to as a steam wool-carding factory. Employees were paid $1,200 annually. The carding business was seasonal, since the Minnesota winters were too harsh to sustain a year-round business. Instead, the mill operated from May until November, although a salesroom stayed open all year.

While it's almost certain that a businessman would start keeping books as soon as he opened, the first records found of Klemer's business are in a daybook dated not 1865 but 1867–71. These and consequential daybooks, inventories and ledgers reside at the University Archives at Minnesota State University–Mankato. Stained at the edge and bottom with what may be a sort of oil, the 1867–71 daybook is a simple numbered list of customers, product and payment. Eventually, the archives stopped labeling the daybooks with "Spinning and Carding Department" and marked separate books with inventory and expense ledgers. As Klemer's business grew, his recordkeeping became more extensive.

In 1871, the *Faribault Republican* reported that cotton had been bought in St. Louis. Cotton was more affordable than wool, and it was carded the same. However, the carding factory did not keep producing the cotton batting because, a relative speculated, the supply couldn't be found.

In 1872, Klemer installed a new spinning machine that made yarn. Davis & Furber Machine Company wrote a letter to Frank, Carl's grandson, explaining that Carl bought a self-operating head for a spinning machine. Though these purchases were several years after Minneapolis mills, Carl built his business in Faribault and established himself quite well locally.

Five years after the factory started spinning yarn, four looms were installed and the mill produced its first blanket. Other products were also made. In 1877, wool was worth sixteen cents to eighteen cents per pound. In "History of Faribault Woolen Mills: 1865–1940," Frank wrote, "At that time cotton warps were bought and used in the manufacture of flannel and wool sheeting. In those days of unheated bedrooms, wool sheeting was highly desirable for comfort, even though it contained a few burrs."

A view of Faribault from the courthouse tower, circa 1874. The mill is bottom right with the smokestack. *Rice County Historical Society Collection–Faribault.*

The first blanket made in 1877. *Photo by Jillian Raye Photography, Faribault Woolen Mill Archives.*

For a year, Carl had competition. A former employee, Bernard Fowler, and his brother-in-law started their own carding mill in Faribault in 1876 called the Straight River Woolen Mill. When it closed, Klemer, who must not have had hard feelings, hired Fowler back as a boss carder and spinner. Fowler eventually left the mill again and finished his career as an engineer at local furniture stores.

It wasn't until 1878 that the factory was identified as the Faribault Woolen Mill in a local Faribault newspaper ad.

MINNESOTA MILLS

Though flour and woolen mills in Minneapolis became the most well known, the site of the first woolen carding mill was in St. Anthony, just north of Minneapolis. A gentleman from Massachusetts by the name of David Lewis founded the company, but it only lasted until the 1860s.

In the small village of Cannon Falls, about forty miles southeast of Minneapolis, the first wool yarn, blankets, clothing and other items were produced. M. Hilliard, the founder, didn't stay long, however, and moved to Minneapolis to establish his carding mill behind the North Star Woolen Mill in 1865. According to the book *History of the City of Minneapolis, Minnesota, Part II*, edited by Isaac Atwater, Hilliard was remembered by "old residents." He stayed at that location for three years before moving into the basement of a machine shop that was next to the North Star Woolen Mill. Hilliard stayed there for years. Atwater wrote, "Country visitors to the city took great pleasure in stepping in and looking at the machines in operation, unhindered by the kind hearted operator, who was evidently fond of visitors."

The same year that Carl Klemer bought his carding machine,

> *Charles Kent Clapp & Co., composed of Wm. T. Brown, Daniel W. Coon, Charles K. Clapp, and Henry L. Watson, built the Minneapolis Woolen Mill at the corner of First Street and Sixth Avenue South. The building was 40 x 70 feet, four stories high, and cost the men $45,000. After running the mill a few years, the firm was changed to Clapp, Watson & Coon. In 1875, Charles A. Pillsbury & Co. bought the property. The machinery was taken out and the mill fitted up to manufacture flour, and became the Empire mill.*

An article in the *Minneapolis Tribune* dated January 7, 1868, described the woolen mill competitors, the Minneapolis Woolen Mill and the North Star Woolen Mill. The former's thirty employees produced 300 yards of fabric a day, fully utilizing the mill's ten looms and 720 spindles. North Star Woolen Mill had twice the number of employees, four times as many looms and 1,050 spindles. With this mill's maximum production of 1,600 yards of fabric a day, it appeared to be the stronger of the two. Despite the North Star Woolen Mill success, it went bankrupt in 1876. A waterpower company bought the mill and hired managers to run it. It surged as the top wool blanket manufacturer in the 1920s. The Minneapolis mill closed in 1949, and the mill operation moved to Lima, Ohio.

The Mill City Museum in Minneapolis is the former site of Cadwallader Washburn's A Mill, a seven-story flour mill first built in 1874. Tragedy struck that mill when eighteen employees were killed in an explosion; dry millstones had rubbed each other and ignited flour dust. The ensuing fire destroyed many of the businesses on the banks of the Mississippi and severed the milling business by one-third up to a half. By the time the A Mill was rebuilt in 1880, better flour was made by safer equipment. Technology had replaced stone with steel rollers. "During its heyday, it was said that the mill ground enough flour to make 12 million loaves of bread a day," according to the Minnesota Historical Society. The mill shut down in 1965, and fire engulfed the building in 1991. The Minneapolis Community Development Agency dredged the site, and the Minnesota Historical Society initiated its plans to build the museum. The Mill City Museum opened on September 13, 2003.

Around Minnesota, other mills rose and fell, including Northwestern Knitting Company/Munsingwear, Minneapolis; Minnetonka Mill Company; New Prague Flouring Mill; Hawkeye Mills, Hay Creek, south of Red Wing; Phoenix Flour Mill/Pillsbury Rye Mill, Minneapolis; the Thompson & Williams Mill, Lanesboro; Laird, Norton Co. lumber mill, Winona; George Stiff's Mill, Minnehaha Creek; and Pioneer Lumber Mill, St. Anthony Falls.

Faribault had a strong flour milling presence during this era. The first King Mill was built in 1862 on the west edge of town. In *Then & Now*, Louise Mott, a former Faribault resident whose parents moved to Faribault to escape disease in Illinois, said that "in 1880 there were at least 15 mills between Faribault and Northfield, and Cannon Valley flour commanded the highest prices on the London and New York stock exchanges because of its high quality." Further:

> *In 1865 Alexander Faribault imported two French millers and a special process for milking hard wheat* [making fine flour out of hard wheat], *which was very successful. For a decade, the Cannon River Valley reigned supreme as a flour milling center, but eventually the Washburn Mills in Minneapolis were able to obtain the secret and patent it. The Bean or H.H. King Mill was the last to keep operating in this area.*

BUSINESSES THAT CALLED FARIBAULT HOME

Carl's woolen mill wasn't the only up-and-coming business in Faribault. In 1856, Ernst Fleckenstein, also from Germany, founded his brewery. His family had started brewing beer in Germany back in 1577. In Faribault, however, as *Then & Now* reported, Ernst felt the village "had an abundance of choice grain at hand, as well as a plentiful supply of finest pure artesian well water." In addition, the perfect place for part of his brewery was inside the sandstone caves near the Straight River. Instead of coming to the United States alone like Carl did, Ernst arrived in Faribault with three brothers. But like Carl, Ernst's family—his sons and grandsons— later managed the business.

In 1935, Felix Frederiksen bought the old Fleckenstein Brewery (after a brief stint as a lamp factory for Peterson Art Furniture) and founded Treasure Cave Blue Cheese. It had only one cave at the time, and Frederiksen made cheese from cow's milk instead of goat's. Through the Great Depression and World War II, the Treasure Cave Blue Cheese factory kept open, even when cheese production had to stop. When the factory turned twenty-five, according to *Then & Now*, "there were a hundred or more farmers bringing in milk and taking home whey for their pigs." Today, Caves of Faribault, a subsidiary of Swiss Family Farms, still makes award-winning cheese. It is the only company in the United States that uses a maze of sandstone caves one hundred feet underground to cure and ripen its blue cheese.

Faribault companies that came and went include Ochs Department Store, Schimmel and Nelson Piano Firm, P.J. Gallagher Plumbing Company, Shaft Pierce Shoe Company, Clarine Brothers Greenhouse and Voegel Ice Cream Company. Sellner Manufacturing, founded in 1914 by Herbert Sellner, became famous for its Water-Toboggan Slide and the Tilt-A-Whirl. The company was sold to another manufacturer in Texas in 2011.

On the other hand, some companies survived all these decades and still welcome customers and clients today. Ray Funeral Home started business in 1876 and is now known as Parker Kohl Funeral Home, located across the street from the Cathedral of Our Merciful Savior, the first Episcopal cathedral built in the United States. The Faribault Foods canning company—known as the Northwestern Canning Company when it opened in 1888—is still located in Faribault; it was recently acquired by a company in Mexico. Also in 1888, the Farmer Seed and Nursery Co. on Fourth Street opened; today it serves customers year round. Faribault State Bank, now known as the State Bank of Faribault, was founded in 1919.

Faribault grew significantly, but story after story in *Then & Now* documents how fire—something the Klemers experienced firsthand—destroyed products, businesses and buildings.

CHAPTER 2

RIVERS AND FIRES

In February 1882, the *Faribault Republican* announced that the mill was moving. That summer, wanting a better water supply, Carl Klemer built a new two-story stone mill near the Straight River on Third Street Northeast, which now turns into Ravine Street across the railroad tracks. Those familiar with Faribault can imagine the mill sat just about where the Depot Square office complex is. What might be more difficult to imagine is the Straight River in a channel west of its current location, nearer First Avenue Northeast. The channel was changed to its current location in 1901 to accommodate train tracks. Klemer bought a new loom from the Crompton and Knowles Loom Works in Massachusetts. Another *Republican* article in November 1883 noted that Klemer "illustrated the virtue of perseverance in the face of obstacles and pointed out the good results that flow from enterprise backed by industry and integrity."

The old mill stayed open until the end of the season in 1882. Equipment was moved and the new mill opened for operation in 1883.

Carl Klemer employed six people at the mill, according to an 1884 payroll book. According to Frank Klemer's written history:

> *Only first names were indicated and a mark for each day worked. The highest paid employee, at that time, received the munificent sum of $7.50 per week for sixty hours, or 12½¢ per hour. This man, Mr. Felix Schwehla, evidently was not discouraged by long hours and small pay, for he later*

became the boss weaver, a position he held for about thirty years until his death in 1919.

This decades-long work record at the mill began the theme of employee longevity still found at the company today.

FIRE TIMES THREE

In 1887, Carl Klemer purchased a Westinghouse Automatic forty-horsepower engine to make his mill more productive. Also that year, he added a retail store and warehouse onto the mill. This addition made the mill forty-four feet wide by one hundred feet long. Unfortunately, the first of the mill's fires occurred in August 1888. The fire caught in the basement and caused $7,000 in loss. This fire did not deter Klemer, however, and he continued his business.

Klemer decided to open a retail branch in Fergus Falls, Minnesota, about 225 miles northwest of Faribault, in the spring of 1888. It is not disclosed why this location was chosen. A gentleman by the name of Lyman Smith ran this store, but it did not stay open long. Again, Klemer's business persevered in spite of the failure in Fergus Falls.

The second fire happened in May almost two years after the first, but it wasn't nearly as bad. The boiler room was the site of the fire, which only caused $1,000 in damage.

From Frank Klemer's history:

> *It was about this time that an Englishman visited the mill and stated that the goods made were about the same in price as equal quality made in England. The* Faribault Republican *newspaper used this to point out the fallacy of free traders who claim that tariffs raise the price of goods in this country.*

In February 1892, when Henry was thirty-seven and Ferdinand was thirty-five, their father gave them each one-third interest in the mill. The company became known as C.H. Klemer & Sons. Soon after this transaction, Carl and his wife returned to Germany to visit their families and friends; they stayed for three months, evidently assured that Henry and Ferdinand would take care of the business without problems. As it

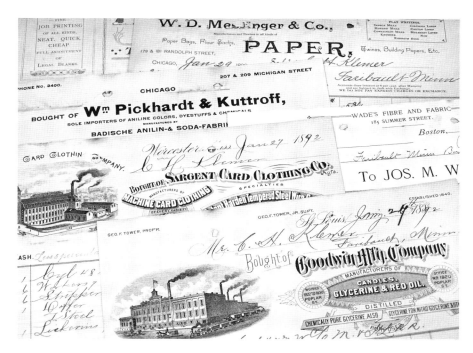

Various receipts from 1892 show the variety of mill supply needs and business locations. *Photo by author, University Archives at Minnesota State University–Mankato.*

turns out, 1892 was a good year for the mill, and as Frank noted, it "had many orders from merchants and during the summer months operated 12 hours per day for six days in the week instead of usual 60 hours per week." By this time, the mill had two sets of equipment, which were run by twenty-five to thirty employees. Copies of receipts from 1892 show a breadth of supplies, from paper to dyestuffs to glycerin that came from around the United States: Chicago, Boston, St. Louis.

Then calamity struck.

On September 7, 1892, at midnight, another fire broke out at the mill. No reason is given for its cause—though a heating or light source was probable—but it didn't really matter. The fire, worsened by the fact that the firefighters' hoses kept bursting, consumed the mill and left a skeleton of stone. A wool warehouse wasn't touched, but the basement became a melted pile of metal. Though the office and salesroom were not destroyed, they bore smoke and water damage. Luckily, the lumber at A.L. Hill's Furniture Company was spared. This fire wasn't as ruinous as the 1878 fire in downtown Faribault that destroyed two banks and ten stores worth $125,000. But for Carl Klemer, with the mill's loss of $24,000 and insurance only covering half, this could have meant the end of his woolen mill business.

A current thirty-six-year employee of the mill speculated that if it weren't for sons Henry and Ferdinand, Carl probably would have sold his equipment and escaped the business. By the time the third fire burned, Carl was over sixty-eight years old. In the late 1800s, this may have felt like ninety. It may well have been Carl's sons who refused to give in. They were still young, and both had taken business classes at a college in Illinois and worked in woolen mills in the East.

From Frank's history:

> After the fire, the owners at first felt that they needed the help of citizens in raising capital to rebuild. A Board of Trade, predecessor of the Chamber of Commerce, called a meeting in the city hall to discuss the matter of forming a stock company. The owners stated that they thought $40,000 would be needed to rebuild and furnish working capital and agreed to subscribe one fourth of this. A committee consisting of Dr. C.H. Wagner, George Pease and A.E. Haven was appointed to confer with the Klemers to see what could be done….Naturally, the Klemers felt that if Faribault could help outsiders financially to start enterprises local people knew nothing about, the town should do something for a business whose operations and management they were acquainted with.

Though Carl, Henry and Ferdinand cleaned up the site of the fire, they ended up buying a small flour mill on the Cannon River. This location became the site of the current mill. This purchase was made mere weeks after the third fire. P.A. Theopold bought the burned site with the condition that the store building remain for several years.

The new site on the Cannon River offered the needed water source and plenty of room to build a woolen mill after the old flour mill was torn down. By October 26, 1892, the new site was prepared for building. The Klemer family chose to build the new mill with brick, which was made locally by E. Kaul. One thousand bricks cost seven dollars. The new building was wider but shorter than the old mill at fifty-two feet by eighty-four feet and was also two stories high. Then a two-story addition was built for the picker house and storage, and a warehouse and other miscellaneous buildings joined the new mill property. A timber dam already existed when the new woolen mill was built.

Inside the mill, the Klemers placed eight looms, four spinning mules and two sets of carding machines. A forty-eight-inch water wheel churned up water in eight to ten feet of the Cannon River for the mill's power. As in its beginning, the mill only produced batting and yarn in early spring 1893, but by August, the mill was again making cloth. Sadly, Carl's wife, Fredricka, did not live to see the rebirth of the mill; she passed away in January 1893 at sixty-five years of age.

DAM, DEATH AND DECEMBER

As if "baptism by fire" was the mill's new mantra, the company experienced a small fire, its fourth, in 1893. Fortunately, it did no damage, only demonstrated that stretching a fire hose 1,750 feet to the nearest hydrant was too far. Though Frank didn't make a note of it, one can assume this problem was remedied in haste.

By 1894, the Klemers had decided to replace the wooden dam with a new stone dam. This twelve-foot structure continued to harvest the Cannon River's strength for the mill's power source.

The family hired Olaf Hanson, an architect and graduate of what was then called the Minnesota School for the Deaf, to construct a building to house offices and a store in 1895. The chosen location was north of the original mill and to the west of Carl's home. Eventually, the side of the building had a small painted sign that read "Office of Faribault Woolen Mill." Though the name "Klemer" no longer appears on the top of the building toward the street, the building still stands. A large mural with "Welcome to HISTORIC DOWNTOWN FARIBAULT, RICE COUNTY, MN," an oval with downtown buildings, "A National Register Historic District" and antique-looking swirls is painted on its gray-beige side. Carl's wooden carding shop behind the Klemer building no longer stands, of course; a parking lot takes up that former space with cars from the law enforcement building to the south.

Because of the bitter Minnesota winters, Carl's mill also ran seasonally. In January 1895, the Klemers built a small gristmill on the property. Frank Klemer wrote, "This was operated for several winters during slack season of the woolen mill, thereby making use of the waterpower that otherwise would have gone to waste."

Though a Klemer family relative isn't sure how they met, Carl and Anna E. Widmer married in Oedbolt, Iowa, in April 1897, when Carl was seventy-three years old. It is unknown how long she lived or where

The Klemer building, circa mid-1890s. The original mill is behind it (right side of photo).
Rice County Historical Society Collection–Faribault.

she is buried. Two Klemer plots are located at Maple Lawn Cemetery in Faribault. A massive gravestone has Carl H. on one half and Anna E. on the other. Anna's death is listed as 1893, four years *before* she married Carl. One might presume that the gravestone is supposed to bear Fredricka's name instead, which would lead to another question: where is Anna? To be researched another time.

For reasons undisclosed, the mill did not have the same success in the late 1890s as it had in the early 1890s. It proved to be a turning point for Ferdinand, who left to become a manager at a wheat elevator in Dundas, a tiny village about eleven miles northeast of Faribault. Fortunately for the Klemers and for the mill, he returned to Faribault within a year.

Even with trouble, employees remained at the mill. The iconic photograph of the Faribault Woolen Mill employees in 1895 has Henry standing in the middle; perhaps Ferdinand was in Dundas at the time. The men are on the left, while the women are on the right. A large tear in the original photograph is stopped at the bottom by tape, as if it's a symbol of the mill's resilience and fortitude to continue, even if marred.

By the turn of the century, more and more consumers were buying clothes already made, "so in 1901," Frank wrote, "the management decided to operate a clothing factory in connection with the mill. Sewing machines were installed in the Fourth Street building, and for several years men's wool

The first-known photo of the new Cannon River mill with employees and H.F. Klemer (middle, black suit) in 1895. *Rice County Historical Society Collection–Faribault.*

shirts and pants were sold to the trade." The mill supplied the power for the sewing machines, running a power line all the way from the Cannon River site to Fourth Street, a distance of almost two miles, straight south down Second Avenue Northwest. In 1903, cloth and blanket production had reached 117,000 yards, up from 16,000 yards seventeen years prior. Also in 1903, the mill bought a new dryer and boiler.

The following comes from the registration form for the National Register of Historic Places:

> *A half story was added to the dye house addition close to the river and a new waterwheel with a larger house was added by 1904. The dam was also modified and the south shore of the Cannon River was excavated, bringing it much closer to the mill building, probably to accommodate the tailrace on the new waterwheel. A small bleach house and a waste house were located west of the mill near the river.*

On March 31, 1904, at eighty years old, Carl Klemer, the founder of what became an international business, died and was buried in Maple Lawn Cemetery. He came full circle to his roots—one neighboring gravestone, tall and marbled white with vines of lichen, has births and deaths, as well as scripture, etched forever in German.

Frank Klemer, who had returned to Faribault two months before Carl's death, joined the mill after Carl died, bringing with him his civil engineering experience gained at a Minnesota university. Frank became the secretary of the mill, Ferdinand was the president and Henry was the vice-president and treasurer when, in December 1905, the business was incorporated under the Faribault Woolen Mill Company name. According to Frank's accounts, the capital paid was $85,900, while the *Minneapolis Journal* notes in its "New Incorporations" section on December 28, 1905, that it was $100,000. Felix Schwehla, the boss weaver, also joined the management team. Frank noted that the mill "had thirteen looms and other machinery in proportion" at the time of this incorporation.

For the first time ever in its history, the mill offered the public stock in the company in February 1906. The only shares sold were to a few employees and to a Minneapolis textile broker. "Those were the trust busting days of Theodore Roosevelt," Frank wrote, "and perhaps local citizens had the same idea as expressed by one retired farmer who, when solicited to buy stock, said the only kind of stock he bought was dehorned stock."

A NEW FAMILY NAME JOINS THE MILL

Not only were the Klemer boys busy with the mill, but they also participated in politics. Henry was a city alderman for several terms in the first decade of the new century, while Ferdinand served as a Rice County representative from 1910 to 1912. Recordkeeping seemed to be of utmost importance to the Klemer family; tax returns, inventories and check registers were but some of thousands of documents, books and files found in the Faribault Woolen Mill Archives and the University Archives at Minnesota State University–Mankato.

The brothers were also busy being fathers—Henry had one son and five daughters, while Ferdinand's children were practically opposite: four sons and one daughter. It is rumored that one of Henry's daughters, Addie, was born with Down syndrome. An English physician, John Landon Down, published a paper about this syndrome in 1866, but it was not until 1959 that the French physician Jérôme Lejeune determined it was a condition concerning chromosomes. The Klemers probably never knew what made their daughter different from the other children. Sadly, Addie only lived to age twenty-six and is buried near her grandfather.

Right: An example of mill inventory recordkeeping from 1908 and 1909. *Faribault Woolen Mill Archives.*

Below: Walter and Frank Klemer, grandsons of Carl. *Photo by Jillian Raye Photography, Faribault Woolen Mill Archives.*

Out of the other ten children, only Walter, Ferdinand's son, showed enthusiasm about the textile business. Walter had gone to Philadelphia to take a class at its textile school. He also gained experience working at other mills, including the North Star Mill located in Minneapolis. It was here that Walter met Edward "Ed" A. Johnson. Ed's experience at the North Star Mill began as a record clerk, but in the next eleven years, he moved up the ranks to become the factory superintendent.

In 1912, at age twenty-six, Walter returned to Faribault from Minneapolis, eager to apply his textile knowledge to his family's woolen mill business; he wanted to expand the blanket production and shift away from clothes.

Ed Johnson eventually joined Walter in Faribault, and their experience "enabled the mill to make blankets that were more attractive and saleable than those previously made," Frank wrote. In a 1980 article from *Corporate Report*, the author noted that Ed and Walter "immediately intensified the specialization of all-wool, fine-quality blankets, curtailing the production of less profitable clothing, piece goods and yarn."

Unfortunately, in part because of the world war brewing, business at the Faribault Woolen Mill was not going well. The worst year was 1914, the first year of World War I. Frank wrote:

> *The senior officers of the company, F.L. and H.F. Klemer, were getting discouraged and wanted to get out of the business…In 1913, the senior officers made a contract to turn over the management of the business to the three junior directors, E.A. Johnson, W.F. Klemer, and F.M. Klemer, and above a certain renumbertion* [sic] *for themselves, to turn over the balance of the profits to the younger men and to sell their stock to the latter as fast as the young men could buy it. Mr. Johnson and Walter were in charge of manufacturing and buying, while the writer* [Frank] *was office manager in charge of sales, credits, and accounting.*

It is interesting to note that Frank mentioned that the mill tried to retain superintendents from mills in the East, but they "did not seem to be able to make a profitable showing in a Western mill." Moreover, "the mill has always found that foremen educated and brought up from the ranks of their employees have been more efficient than those brought in from the East." Frank then listed those foremen: F.W. Bultman, foreman of weaving; Alfred Frechette, foreman of spinning; Fred C. Jones, foreman of dyeing and finishing; and Earl R. Steele, foreman of carding. Frank wrote his history in 1940 and mentioned the above foremen having been

Grandson Robert "Pete" Johnson, son Robert "Bob" Johnson, and Edward "Ed" Johnson from the mill's partner family. *Photo by Jillian Raye Photography, Faribault Woolen Mill Archives.*

Agnes Robertson, a mill employee, made sure she left her mark by etching her name in brick in 1914. *Photo by Jillian Raye Photography.*

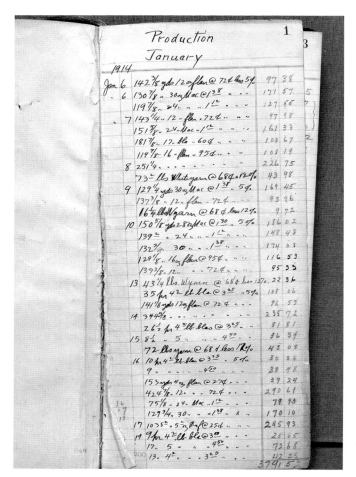

The mill's production record book from 1914 to 1927 opened to the first page, January 1, 1914. *Photo by author, University Archives at Minnesota State University–Mankato.*

employed since the early or mid-1910s, adding to the trend of the mill's veteran employees.

Frank also wrote about other employees who had been with the mill for twenty years or more and were still employed at the time of his written history: Theresa O'Brien, Carl Pommeranz, Charles Zeamann, John H___ (unreadable) and Margaret Cahill. Frank credited blanket salesman Mr. M.J. Whitfield, of Cedar Rapids, Iowa, for an increase in business in 1915. In fact, until his death in 1932, Whitfield was the leading salesman for the mill. The application for the National Register of Historic Places stated that Whitfield landed the contract with the U.S. Army.

Chapter 3

BLANKETING THE
TROOPS AND THE NATION

B y 1917, business was looking up for the mill. That lasted only until the United States joined the fighting in World War I. Frank wrote that "the government took control of wool and other raw materials. Our mill was given contracts to make olive drab army blankets at prices fixed by the army quartermaster and was allotted wool at prices also fixed by the government." Despite the price fixing, the mill made 100,000 olive drab (OD) army blankets. One of those, hand monogrammed, is in the mill's archives.

On the other hand, making so many blankets for the military did help the mill learn about mass production, and blankets didn't change like fashion constantly did, which kept sales more stable. Also, this military contract was actually in addition to another military customer the mill had starting making blankets for in 1915—the cadets at West Point. Even today, the mill continues its tradition of making wool blankets for those who serve the country.

In January 1918, Henry Klemer, Carl's oldest son, passed away at the age of sixty-three. After this, the younger Klemers and Johnsons bought the older generation's stock and elected new officers: Frank became president, Walter became vice-president and Ed Johnson became the secretary and treasurer. Just four years after his brother's death, at the age of sixty-six, Ferdinand Klemer died.

With the experience of making one kind of blanket for the U.S. Army, the mill officers decided to focus on "the idea of making only one quality, size and weight blanket." The mill made double-fold plaid blankets in a variety of colors and sold a pair of them for $8.00 to $10.50 wholesale. Postwar prices peaked

This rare photograph was taken between 1920 and 1922. The advertisement on the wall uses the easier phonetic spelling of the town. *Meyer Family Archive.*

around 1920 before commodities collapsed in 1921. By 1922, the wholesale price of the blankets dropped to about $5.50 a pair. Eventually, a variety of blankets was being made, and it was decided to stop the production of the double-fold blankets. During this time, blankets were also made for motels, hospitals, institutions, sanatoriums and Native American schools.

ADDING ON

From the time of incorporation in 1905 until 1915, the mill bought six additional lots, which provided room to build a three-story addition in 1922–23. Because of the extra space, the mill purchased eight more looms from the Daniel Boone Mill in Chicago after it closed. Carding, spinning and other machines were also bought in order to balance the mill's production capabilities. In 1905, the mill had thirteen looms and three sets of carding machines. By 1923, those numbers had increased to thirty-two looms and seven sets of carding machines. Frank wrote:

> *No outside capital was used to finance these additions to buildings and equipment, so the profits of the business were used for this purpose and*

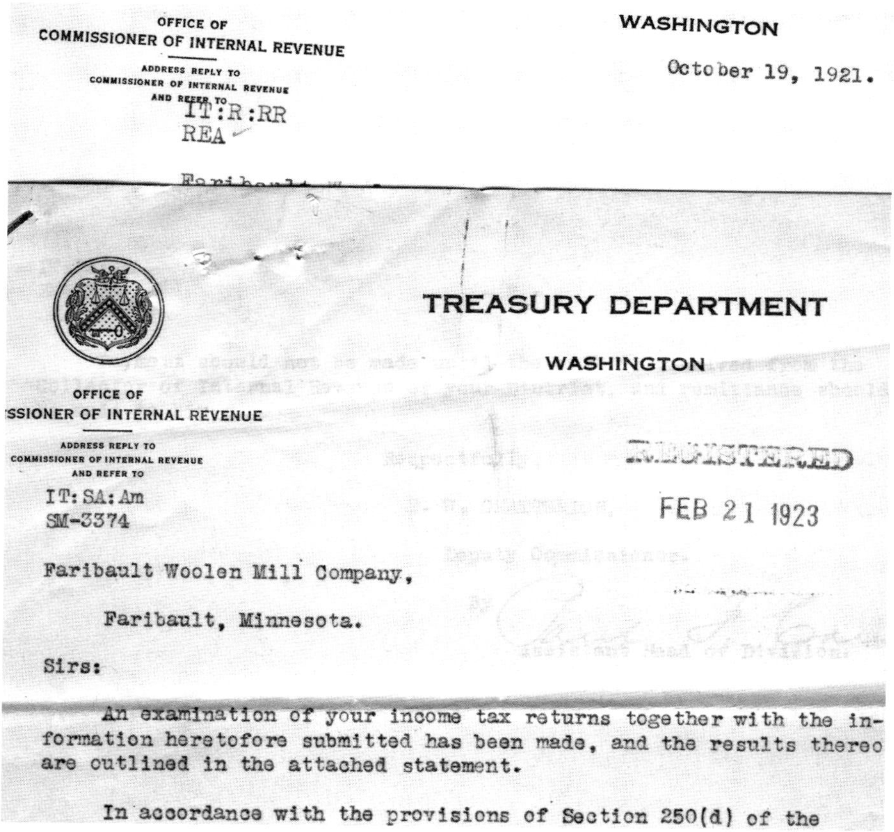

OFFICE OF
COMMISSIONER OF INTERNAL REVENUE

ADDRESS REPLY TO
COMMISSIONER OF INTERNAL REVENUE
AND REFER TO
IT:R:RR
REA

WASHINGTON

October 19, 1921.

TREASURY DEPARTMENT

WASHINGTON

OFFICE OF
SSIONER OF INTERNAL REVENUE

ADDRESS REPLY TO
COMMISSIONER OF INTERNAL REVENUE
AND REFER TO
IT: SA: Am
SM-3374

REGISTERED

FEB 21 1923

Faribault Woolen Mill Company,

Faribault, Minnesota.

Sirs:

An examination of your income tax returns together with the information heretofore submitted has been made, and the results thereo are outlined in the attached statement.

In accordance with the provisions of Section 250(d) of the

Correspondence with the Treasury Department in Washington, D.C., during the 1920s. *Faribault Woolen Mill Archives.*

stock issued in the form of stock dividends to the stockholders. In addition to $100,000 of common stock originally authorized, a similar amount of preferred stock was issued during the 1920s to take care of these expansions. In January 1927, the office and salesroom in the Klemer Building at 127–129 West 4th Street was discontinued and moved to a mill addition then completed.

Though Carl had depended on water for his business, first from the Straight River and then the Cannon, it was no longer needed for power. Most likely not many years after the photograph of the mill on stilts was taken in the early 1920s, the use of water power was stopped and the equipment taken out of the building. The mill then began using steam power to generate electricity.

Although this photograph is blurry, it's an extremely rare view of the mill on stilts between 1920 and 1922. *Meyer Family Archive.*

This employee photograph from 1925 is only the right third of a panorama portrait. *Faribault Woolen Mill Archives.*

In the 1930s, the next generation of Klemers and Johnsons joined the company. Robert "Bob" E. Johnson, son of Ed, graduated from Shattuck School in Faribault. His college years were spent at the Wharton School of Finance at the University of Pennsylvania and the University of Minnesota. Robert "Bob" Wadsworth Klemer, Carl's great-grandson, graduated from Faribault High School and attended the University of Minnesota. Like his cousin Walter, Bob Klemer also went to the Philadelphia Textile School. It was here that he completed the woolen and worsted course. (Worsted is tightly twisted yarn spun from wool fiber.) The mill hired Bob Johnson in 1932 to work in the office assisting Frank. The mill hired Bob Klemer as the assistant superintendent of manufacturing. By 1935, both men had been elected directors of the company. Bob Johnson became secretary of the company; his father, Ed, remained the treasurer.

From 1930 until 1945, a name is repeated in the mill's check registers over and over: Israel Gendler. On September 13, 1930, the mill wrote a check to Gendler for $645.28 for wool. The mill also bought pelts from him. In three days in September 1942, the mill bought almost $28,000 of wool from him. In April of the next year, it was almost three times as much. The mill supported Gendler, who must have been a local farmer, and Gendler supported the mill, a local business.

Though it's not mentioned in Frank's history, the mill shut down temporarily as the nation grappled with the Great Depression. In Jeff Jarvis and LaVonne Brick's *Book of Memories*, a daughter wrote, "My father, Bill Mapes, was one of the old faithful workers at the mill for 43 years. When the mill closed for a time in the '30s, Dad was hired as a night watchman. He did receive a check in those bad times. He never forgot the kindness of the Klemers to give him this job to keep our family going."

On a humorous note, the *Faribault Journal* ran a short article in the spring of 1936 about Louis Schwichtenberg, who was an engineer at the mill. When he went into work, he "saw a nice pickerel swimming before his eyes. The fact is that it was a real pickerel and Mr. Schwichtenberg caught it, too. The water from the millpond had risen so much from the heavy rains that it had backed into the plant to a depth of fifteen inches."

The first four automatic looms made by Crompton and Knowles were purchased by the mill in 1937. Eventually, the mill installed twenty-five of these looms. The next several years saw the mill's equipment move from spinning mules to spinning frames. Both mules and frames are multi-spindle machines, but the mule has a moving carriage, while the frame stays in one

An older frame spinner machine from a lower angle. Bobbins are on the bottom. *Faribault Woolen Mill Archives.*

place, taking up less room. Assuredly, the extra room and additional frames increased productivity.

In February 1938, the mill decided to give the City of Faribault all the land to the north of Cannon River. This land included the millpond and dams. The decision was made because the city was planning to design Alexander Park across the pond on the north side, and the management felt the pond could be used by Faribault citizens. "Perhaps it should not be classed entirely as a gift, as the city paid previous year's taxes on the property," Frank wrote, "and agreed to let the mill have the use of the water for power and industrial purposes." In addition, as a current veteran employee pointed out, the mill would no longer have to be responsible for the upkeep and liability of the dams.

In order to keep up with orders as the nation clawed out of the Depression, the mill installed an efficient engine generator in 1938. A year later, it bought a stainless steel dyeing machine. With expertise and equipment, employees at the mill manufactured 400,000 pounds of blankets.

Another family member joined the mill in the summer of 1939. Boyd Sartell, Walter Klemer's son-in-law (married to Adelle Klemer), started working in sales and wool buying. He brought with him ten years of experience working for Standard Oil Company.

BLANKETS NEAR AND FAR

Twenty-three years after the first order of blankets for troops in war, the mill was contracted again in October 1940 to make olive drab army blankets for World War II soldiers. On the mill's website timeline, it is reported that "civilian volunteers flood[ed] to the mill" in 1941 and assisted in this endeavor and "devote[d] their own time and sweat to the mill, helping to fill each and every order." Five life-changing years later, the mill had manufactured what was comparable to almost 250,000 blankets for the military (some cloth had been used for sleeping bags instead of blankets). Though the laws during the war restricted how much wool could be blended into civilian merchandise, the company added other fiber in order to still produce some products for civilians.

In *Book of Memories*, the daughter of employee William "Bill" Kruse wrote that her dad "was drafted during the war but was sent home because blankets were considered 'essential' to the war." Bill Mapes's daughter wrote, "Never to be forgotten is the Klemer family who shut down orders to provide blankets for our troops during World War II."

Besides providing blankets and cloth for the military internationally, the company had a strong following in stores around the United States. In the late '30s through October 1940, the following stores carried Faribault Woolen Mill blankets, then known as "Faribo" blankets, a logo created by Ed Johnson: Los Angeles's May Company and Bullock's; San Francisco's Emporium; New York's R.H. Macy & Company; Boston's R.H. Stearns & Company and Filene's; Chicago's Carson Pirie Scott Company and Marshall Field & Company; California's Hales Stores; and undisclosed Twin Cities department stores, which may have included Dayton's, Donaldson's, Young-Quinlan, Powers and Field-Schlick. Frank wrote, "Very little has been sold to the mail order and chain stores, as it is felt that trade with independent merchants is on a higher quality basis and is more dependable year after year."

Frank Klemer ended his written 1865–1940 history with this overview of the mill:

> *The record of the business had not been a brilliant one of phenomenal growth but on the contrary one of plodding along conservatively, feeling its way, letting others experiment with new ideas or machinery before they were adopted by us. This method was not one to produce large profits, but it did prevent large losses and enabled the business to remain in solvent condition and always able to pay its obligations promptly. The mill has tried to make good merchandise and treat its employees and customers in a fair and just*

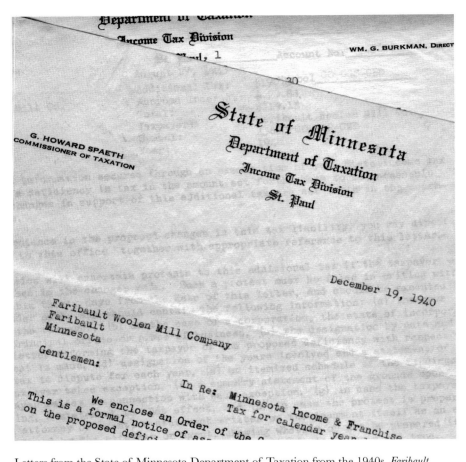

Letters from the State of Minnesota Department of Taxation from the 1940s. *Faribault Woolen Mill Archives.*

manner, has never, in its long existence, had any labor trouble with its own employees. Since 1919, it has carried group life insurance on all employees who have been in its service six months or more. The management takes a friendly interest in personal affairs of its employees, who are encouraged to bring their complaints and troubles direct to the office or to their foremen.

The Faribault Woolen Mill Company moved forward.

Chapter 4

POSTWAR CHANGES

Immediately after the attack on Pearl Harbor on December 7, 1941, Bob Klemer was called into service. After three months of training, he was assigned to Washington, D.C., but was transferred in November 1942 to the Philadelphia Quartermaster Depot. Here, he wrote, he "assumed duties in the Procurement Division in connection with the inspection of Quartermaster contracts for woolen and worsted materials and blankets." Two years later, he was transferred to Boston, where he was in charge of inspecting the contracts for New England mills. After the war, he returned to Faribault as the mill's production superintendent with even more wool experience on his résumé. In 1949, he was elected president, the fourth generation of Klemers.

Jeff Jarvis wrote an entry for Conrad Stearns's page in *Book of Memories*:

> *Conrad and others left for World War II, which decimated the woolen mill's workforce. The mill still had thousands of blankets to make for the military. All around the country, women broke out of typical family roles to fill jobs once occupied by men who left for the war. If not for this female workforce, typified by "Rosie the Riveter," an American cultural symbol of women who worked wartime jobs, G.I.s would not have had warm blankets in foxholes.*

Perhaps as a consequence of a world war when boundaries changed and opened, the mill developed international relationships. Before the war, the

These envelopes and shipping receipt from the 1940s were found in one of the mill's warehouses in 2015. *Photo by author.*

mill depended on domestic wool, mostly from farms in its home state of Minnesota, as well as its neighbor to the south, Iowa. After the war, however, the mill found the merino wool from New Zealand to be of higher quality; because of that country's vegetation and because the sheep there were bred for the wool and not as a source of meat, the fibers had exceptional color, length and cleanliness. The company manufactured both domestic and international wool starting in 1945. This shift may be one of the reasons the checks to local farmer Israel Gendler stopped.

As in the past, much of the profits the mill generated went back into the company. In fifteen years' time after World War II ended, eight building projects doubled the square feet of the plant, and new machinery purchases increased significantly. Bob took over writing the mill's history from his father and documented specifics in his first addendum:

> *Wool Dusters and Openers, 48" Hunter Four Bowl Wool Scouring Train, Wool Stock Dryer, Stainless Steel Stock Dye machines, Pit Feed and Squeeze Rolls, Mixing and Burr Pickers, complete 60" Cards and*

additional Tape Condensers for others, Peraltas, Spinning frames Automatic Rewinders, Coner, Automatic Crompton & Knowles Looms and Warner & Swasey Weaving machines, Warp Dressing machines, Inspection and Burling Machine, Fulling Mills, Cloth Washers, Squeeze Rolls and Piece Dying Machines, Nappers, Cloth Shear and Semi-Decater, and Blanket Binding machines. In addition, some of the most modern office machinery and equipment has been installed.

In the years after the war, the mill continued to expand its product line and advertise around the nation as much as possible. The company did not want to become a statistic—yet another woolen mill to shut down. According to Bob Klemer, only forty-five midwestern mills remained in Minnesota, Wisconsin, Iowa, Illinois, Michigan, Indiana and Ohio in 1945. In 1886, there had been eight hundred woolen mills in the north central states.

And advertise it did, using the "Faribo" logo. Magazines such as *New Yorker, Living for Young Homemakers, House Beautiful* and *Holiday* carried the ads. Meanwhile, salesmen traveled the nation to sell the woolen goods, and the company

These newspaper ad templates are from 1952. *Photo by author, Faribault Woolen Mill Archives.*

wrote contracts with hotels, government institutions, the military and others. Newspaper templates from the early 1950s found in the Faribault Woolen Mill Archives had such wording as "Traditionally in good taste," "An invitation to beauty" and "Faribo blankets…the perfect gift for every bride!"

From *Book of Memories*, a woman whose daughter worked at the mill wrote:

> *I graduated from Faribault High School in 1948…I remember well whenever anyone would get married, we would each put in about a $1.00 and go together to get a woolen mill blanket for a wedding gift. It had to be for a "big" bed, which back then, of course, was a full-size bed. I wonder how many of those newly married couples still have their woolen mill blankets? I know I still have some in my house.*

CHANGES APLENTY

Boyd, Walter's son-in-law, liked to experiment. In *Book of Memories*, his daughter claimed that he was "always bringing home ideas, like the day he cut a hole in the middle of a fringed robe to make new shawls for me and my friends." Robert "Pete" Johnson, Ed's grandson, acknowledged that Boyd invented the Pak-a-Robe, a product introduced in 1949 and sold through the 1980s. Even President Eisenhower commended the mill for producing such an "ingenious gift." For the mill's 150th anniversary, the company designed a limited edition.

A 1952 radio script found in the Faribault Woolen Mill vault praised the new product:

> *ANNOUNCER: When you are choosing a gift, don't you want to pick one that you will be proud to give…a gift that the receiver will use for many years to come and remember you gratefully every time he uses it? The perfect answer to these gift problems is the beautiful, versatile Faribo PAK-A-ROBE, the gift that knows no season, that is equally at home at the beach, in the car or plane, at the stadium, or on hunting and fishing trips. Snug in its own zippered carrying case of leather-like plastic and robe matching plaid is a Faribo all-wool Robe in one of our four brilliant Tartan plaids…Hunters' Red, Deepwater Blue, Saddle Brown, or Forest Green. As a cushion or as a robe, in transit or after it's arrived…the Faribo PAK-A-ROBE is the most talked about beauty on the market today. See them today at (name of store) where they are selling for just (price).*

Sadly, part of the mill's changes had to do with death. Walter died in June 1952 at age sixty-six; his cousin Frank, eight years older, died in January 1953. In his first history addendum, Bob Klemer made sure to mention the foremen who had been such an instrumental part of the mill's success; a few had died, while others retired. Three of them had worked at the mill for thirty-four years; Louis Schwichtenberg, a plant engineer, had worked at the business for thirty-seven years; and Fred C. Jones had put in forty-six years at the mill at the time of his retirement. Theresa O'Brien, mentioned in Frank's history, had become Mrs. Ryan but still worked at the mill after forty-seven years. Bob mentioned several more employees with decades-long experience. He wrote:

> The company's relationships with its employees have always been on the friendliest basis. We are now approaching our 100th Anniversary without ever having a strike or any serious labor disturbance in all of our history. In about 1937, the employees formed their own independent organization, the Faribault Woolen Mill Workers Guild, and have continued to hold this organization intact to the present day in spite of efforts from other organizations to seek to organize and represent the employees. Contract negotiations with the Guild have been most amicable and the employees have gained many fringe benefits as well as wage increases, which have helped improve their status.

Tom Klemer, Carl's great-great-grandson who worked at the company, said this about the employees:

> The mill always retained their employees and treated them well. But it was almost a necessity because with the textile industry, you can't go find a weaver. You can't go find a spinner. You can't go find a card mechanic. So, you know if we had moved to the Southeast when a lot of the textile industry did back in the 1940s and '50s, maybe it would've been different, but that's not in our family's make-up, you know, to go where the cheaper labor is or where there's incentives. One of the competitive challenges we had was to continually groom our replacements, whether they be mechanics or…it's a specialized industry. About the only place where we could have people walk in and start up are probably some of the support staff or office or sewers because back in the day, a lot more people sew than they do now. To get them up to speed, just a little bit of training. Most of the other departments, you can't find a guy who knows how to dye wool.

This photo was taken at a national sales meeting at the mill in 1955. *Faribault Woolen Mill Archives.*

As textile companies experimented with other fibers to manufacture their blankets, so did the employees at the Faribault Woolen Mill. Nine years after World War II ended, Bob Klemer noted in his first addendum, the mill produced blankets made of 100 percent Acrilan made by the Chemstrand Corporation. The DuPont Company made Orlon, and the mill tried making blankets with nylon. Of course, switching from all-wool production to synthetic materials meant the mill had to change its procedures. The dyeing and finishing procedures were the most affected. In fact, the Warner & Swasey weaving machines were sold after only six years; the performance was poor, and the maintenance costs didn't justify the expense.

An article from a newspaper section called "Minnesota's Famous Trademarks" dated September 19, 1954, noted that "Loomed by Faribo of Minnesota" helped identify the company on labels and advertisements. A total of 160 employees worked at the mill at that time and were capable of producing six thousand blankets and robes a week. "A million pounds of wool is used yearly," the article claimed.

In September 1954, Mary Glor (married name Boudreau) was hired. She was eighteen years old, and many of her relatives, including her sister, worked at the mill. A position opened in the weave shop, and her sister got her the job. Mary recalled working with a lot of older people her first day.

Mary Boudreau, an employee for sixty-one years, shows how she used to tie each strand of yarn on the loom. *Photo by Jillian Raye Photography.*

"They were just lovely," Mary said. "They taught me a lot, and they were patient with my learning."

Her first job was magazine filler, eight hours of replacing empty bobbins and helping shuttles run smoothly.

"You kept busy. You kept moving," she said.

A year later, the lead in the weave shop was killed in a car accident, and Mary was told to move to that position. At that time, it was called the floor lady, but it's called the lead hand today. When she first started the position, she had to hand tie all the warp yarn on the looms.

"I got up to, I could tie 2,880 ends in less than two hours," Mary said. "By hand."

Today, a tying machine completes the task. Mary claimed, however, that the machine isn't any faster than she was.

"Dick Klemer, one of the owners? He'd say, 'We don't need a tying machine. We got Mary.'"

As business continued to grow, the management team felt it had to keep making improvements to its products in order to ensure customers of long-lasting warmth and quality features. Bob Klemer wrote, "It was the first blanket mill in the country to experiment with, adopt, and market blankets with several new permanent mothproofing compounds. These proved to be most effective and were the first mothproofing compounds to be certified as permanent by the U.S. Department of Agriculture." This development was in 1956. The mill also wanted to figure out how to prevent the wool from shrinking so much and continued researching new procedures.

At the end of 1956, the navy contracted the mill to make 66,666 blankets for its sailors.

Short newspaper articles kept at the Minneapolis Central Library shared three stories from the late 1950s. The first described the mill's Duf-L-Robe, "a combination robe, foot warmer and cushion," which received a Hess Design Award recognizing its design and use. The second stated that the company had joined the Woolens and Worsteds of America, Inc., "an association which is conducting a nationwide promotion of American-made wool products." The third article described the production of the Pak-a-Cooler, "which combines a portable food and beverage cooler with a blanket robe in a zippered case."

In 1959, when the mill depended more on Northern States Power Company, the steam engines and electrical generators were taken out of the mill. This change was inevitable and made the mill more of an impressive manufacturer.

For years, newspapers around the nation proclaimed bad news: this mill closes, that mill's workers go on strike, another mill finds its wages under a wrecking ball. Good news was sparse. Someone at the mill started a scrapbook, found in the Faribault Woolen Mill Archives, that documented many of these headlines and stories from the late 1940s until the mid-1950s. Most have retained their original black-and-white newsprint, while others have dried glue seeping through like stains. One article declared itself in French, the cognate of "terminee" in the headline so close to "terminal," as in "end." Maybe someone at the mill in small-town Faribault wanted to faintly trumpet its David side, with Goliath as fate that messed with the mill on Cannon River at times but couldn't knock it down like others.

An article titled "How to Revive a Mill" voiced foreshadowing. Dated November 1, 1954, the article spoke of a mill in Winooski, Vermont, a textile factory that had employed 2,400 people during World War II but shut down because of financial loss:

It is the solution of resident-ownership, not absentee ownership, for one thing. The new owners, in two Winooski corporations, will be local people rather than disinterested stockholders from "all over the lot." Their interest in seeing the mill operate efficiently and profitably will be, therefore, far more intimate and immediate than ever could be the case when small blocks of stock are owned by strangers, so to speak, whose chief concern is that dividends will be declared at regular intervals.

Further, the Winooski plan "sounds like a community venture—like a community investment in the whole community's well-being. It may prove to be an ideal solution."

THE GLORY YEARS OF THE '60S

By the early 1960s, Richard "Dick" Klemer, son of Frank and Bob's younger brother by sixteen years, had become plant superintendent. This step was after he, too, graduated from the Philadelphia Textile School and worked his way up for a decade. Boyd and Bob Johnson were vice-presidents, Elmer Schultz was secretary and production manager, Tom Kaul was sales manager and Wayne Hultquist was treasurer and office manager. When Hultquist left in 1962, he was replaced by Fran Miller, who was hired as controller and office manager.

Carl's great-grandson Robert "Bob" Klemer, Walter's son-in-law Boyd Sartell and Carl's great-grandson Richard "Dick" Klemer. *Photo by Jillian Raye Photography, Faribault Woolen Mill Archives.*

Always keeping the customer in mind, the company produced a blanket in 1960 that it termed "carefree" because the fabric could be washed again and again. An advertisement found in the mill's archives asked consumers if they could tell which of the two blanket samples had been washed 120 times. (The samples were lifted to see the answer.)

An outrageous "carefree" event happened in 1960 when a "carefree" child most likely released the brake in his/her mother's car while she was in the mill's retail store. Whatever happened sent both car and child into the reservoir. Charlie Champlin, vice-president of special markets, wrote in his 1990 mill history update: "The child was unhurt and the car fine until the tow truck ripped the undercarriage when trying to pull it over the retaining wall."

Coincidentally, the mill bought a cabin and two outbuildings near Bemidji, Minnesota, in 1961 and named it Carefree Lodge. All three buildings needed major remodeling, but the company finished the projects with its own labor in its own time. Its purpose was for employees, salesmen and customers to use and enjoy.

Another strategy the mill had for encouraging business was reaching out to schools and other learning organizations. A copied letter signed by Richard Klemer, superintendent, at a time when the phone number for the mill was "Edison 4-6444," explained in layman terms how the mill worked. This one-and-a-half-page document outlined each step of the process. In the document, Dick diplomatically described scouring: "When we first receive the raw wool, it comes into our plant right from the sheep's back. As this wool is full of dirt and grease, the first thing we do is wash it. Sometimes wools will lose as much as half of their weight in scouring out this dirt and grease."

A *Commercial West* article from May 1965 stated, "But conservative attitudes toward growth, and concern with a sound return to the consumer in exchange for his dollar, have not interfered with the company's enthusiasm for product development or entering new markets." The thermal weave blanket called Lanalaire initially produced in 1964 is one such example of new development that could be used by consumers all year long. In the same article, it stated that sales had increased ten times from what they had been just five decades before. Also important to note was the continued tie with the town of Faribault, as highlighted in the *Commercial West* article:

The company receives offers to move South "almost daily," Klemer says, "but we like it here. Our personnel are highly competent, we've become a part of the community during the past 100 years, and we're close enough to

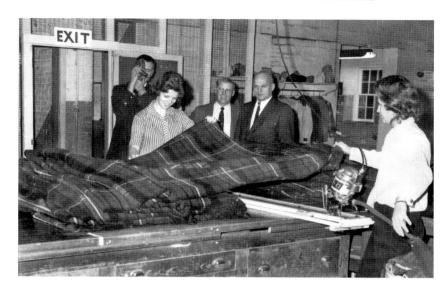

Women cutting yardage into blankets for the 100th anniversary in 1965, a similar scene past and present. *Faribault Woolen Mill Archives.*

A boy and a girl with a blanket made in the mid-1880s, hung for the mill's 100th anniversary in 1965. *Faribault Woolen Mill Archives.*

the Twin Cities (less than an hour's drive) to have the advantages of a big city along with the compensations of small-city living."

Just as Henry and his brother Ferdinand upheld their civic duty, others in the mill's century-old history held city positions or served on the school board in Faribault.

In 1965, one hundred years after Carl decided to try his hand at carding, the Faribault Woolen Mill celebrated its anniversary. The mill opened up the plant to allow manufacturing admirers and woolen-good fans to see firsthand how its products were made. One impressive display was of a blanket with a sign that read, "Produced by Faribo in mid 1880s. Have been used by Miss Nell Foster [her address] for approximately 80 years."

The mill was recognized nationwide for this centenary celebration. Locally, a banquet was held at Faribault High School, where the governor of Minnesota, Karl Rolvaag, spoke to a considerably sized gathering of attendees who had been extensions of the woolen mill family, wool dealers, salesmen and suppliers.

Unfortunately, the inventor who loved to experiment with woolen products, Boyd Sartell, passed away from cancer just before the mill celebrated its centennial. Ed Johnson, whom Walter convinced to move to the Faribault Woolen Mill in the early 1900s, died at the age of eighty-seven three years later.

LASTING IMPRESSIONS

A guest book that sat in the retail store from January 31, 1966, until September 18, 1966, has close to two thousand signatures. Nine of those were from Faribault. Medford, Owatonna and Northfield guests also signed their names. People from forty-four other states visited the mill in those eight months. Visitors from nine countries, the USS *America* and "from Wisconsin in transit for Guam" also traveled to the Faribault Woolen Mill. In August, someone wrote that the Beatles from London, England, had visited. Many people also made glowing comments, while one was honest about the plant tour: "Interesting and noisy."

On February 18, 1967, a blanket customer penned a letter to the sirs at the mill:

Herewith I am returning one of your very fine but well used woolen blankets, the story of which I feel might be of interest to you. Of the thousands of blankets, which your company has manufactured, there are likely few of which you know the history.

On a cold winter night in about 1930, I was driving from Farmington, Minnesota, to my home in Northfield. I was quite discouraged, my youthful, pastoral zeal having been thwarted, because my proposal of a merger of the two Lutheran churches in Farmington had been rejected…

I was not much in the mood to stop to pick up a man beside the road, not knowing if it could be a trick for a hold-up. So I had gone by about half a mile when my conscience convinced me I should go back, which I did. Upon asking the man if I could help him, he identified himself as a salesman for the Faribault Woolen Mills. I had a rope with me, so I towed his car to Northfield and took him home with me for the night.

The next morning we got his car to a garage, and he went on his way after offering to pay, which we declined. Much to our happy surprise a few days later, there came in the mail a beautiful blanket. We were indeed pleased, as this was when salaries for the small town pastor were very small.

In the course of time we adopted five children and had two born to us. We also took other children into our home from time to time. All in the meantime it was the red blanket that was used, both when they were sick and when they were well. There was something special about being wrapped in its comfort.

The letter continued with how the family moved from place to place, still finding comfort in the "Red Blanket." The letter ended:

The Red Blanket says, "A change has come about. I still get a chance to cover up kids, but they are some of the 15 grandchildren, which constitute the new generation. And now I hear my master and mistress say they are going to Viet Nam to set up a child care center, and I just don't believe I can take that trip and see all that suffering, so I am suggesting they give me a one-way ticket to the Faribault Woolen Mills, asking that two blankets be sent along to Viet Nam in my place." The Red blanket says, "Please!"

When we get to Viet Nam with the Faribault blankets, we will send you a photo of them in use.

The Red Blanket and its letter reside in the mill's archives.

After Bob Klemer attended the International Textile Machinery Exhibition in Basel, Switzerland, in 1967, another critical piece of the mill's history ensued. Hearings were held before the Subcommittee on Commerce and Finance of the Committee on Interstate and Foreign Commerce, House of Representatives, Ninetieth Congress. Though the Flammable Fabrics Act had already been passed in 1953, supporters felt it needed to be extended to bedding, upholstery and other fabrics found in the home instead of merely covering clothes. Specifically, the act targeted the synthetic fiber called viscose rayon. The Honorable Albert S. Quie, a representative in Congress from Minnesota who later became governor in the state, testified in person. He read a statement by a father who said a sparkler had ignited his five-and-a-half-year-old daughter's synthetic dress. Representative Quie also brought a statement written by Bob Klemer. Bob wrote of the development of new goods with different synthetic fibers and noted that "wool and mod-acrylic fibers have proven to be the greatest resistance to burning." Bob emphasized how important it was for companies to know the flammability of fibers and how the fabric was constructed in order to protect consumers from such horrible incidences.

The bill passed before the end of 1967. Bob and Minnesota senator Hubert Humphrey flew to Washington, D.C., and witnessed President Lyndon Johnson signing the bill.

CHAPTER 5

BLANKETS GO SKY HIGH

With the Klemers and the Johnsons still at the helm, the Faribault Woolen Mill extended its glory years into the next decade. The '70s presented significant headlines around the world. The tragic: the Cambodian genocide, terrorists at the Olympics, the Jonestown massacre. The troublesome: Three Mile Island nuclear accident, the Iran hostage crisis, Nixon's resignation. The celebratory: the new Disney World with its $3.50 entrance fee, the genesis of *Star Wars* and *Saturday Night Live*, Mother Teresa graced with the Nobel Peace Prize. The triumphant: the United States celebrated its 200th birthday.

In 1971, an engineering firm studied the design and needs of the current Faribault Woolen Mill layout and suggested that it expand, the "largest-ever capital investment and expansion program" in the mill's history, Bob Klemer wrote in his second addendum to the history of the business. A one-story addition was built to the south, which added 37,500 square feet. After a grand-scale move, the carding, spinning and weaving departments occupied the new space. In addition, Bob wrote, "[T]he company purchased four, 3-year-old high spinning frames made by Duesberg-Bosson Company of Belgium and three used Davis and Furber 60-inch carding machines for installation in the new building. Four older spinning frames were demolished at that time."

The same year, Bob returned to the International Textile Machinery Exhibition with his brother, Dick, this time in Paris, where the men bought eight Swiss-made Sulzer Weaving machines that could weave up to six colors. These

These airline time-study notes written in the 1970s helped keep track of production. *Faribault Woolen Mill Archives.*

machines arrived in 1972 after they traveled by freighter from Germany to the scenic port in Duluth on Lake Superior, the massive ship threading through the 1871 canal and under the iconic lift bridge. The weaving machines shifted to railcars to journey to Faribault, and they were in operation by that fall. Bob believed they were the only ones in the nation at that time.

As transportation by airline became more important not only for business travelers but also for those escaping on vacation, the Faribault Woolen Mill secured contracts in 1971 with some of the major airlines at the time, such as United, American, Eastern, Western, National, Republic and Continental. Passengers snuggled in to lightweight wool blankets, naturally flame-resistant, as the planes soared through the sky.

In 1972, G. Charles "Charlie" Champlin joined the mill to provide exclusive business sales and incentives. Bob Klemer wrote, "Our blankets and robes have been used as premiums by many large banks and savings and loan institutions as incentives for savings by depositors. Premium use by industry has also been an important source of sales."

From 1957 until 1972, the mill offered piece-good fabrics sold to women's and men's apparel companies through the Exclusive Fabrics Corporation. John Abt ran this corporation, but the mill decided that since it never reached past 15 percent of the mill's total sales, the company wanted to focus on what it knew best: blankets.

Despite the huge expansion years before, the mill staff felt the wet finishing department was too confined. Another six thousand square feet was built on the west side along the river in 1974, and a new James Hunter cloth dryer was added.

It may never be known if the 1973 oil embargo rattled Bob Klemer enough to do so, but he gathered much of the heritage of the mill—daybooks, receipts, inventories, check registers—and delivered it into the hands of the librarians at the University Archives at Minnesota State University–Mankato. With such irreplaceable items as Carl's daybooks from the first years of his business, Bob must have felt compelled to have them somewhere for safekeeping, just in case something happened at the mill. Boxes and files and books invite the curious, the historians, the devotees.

CRISIS, COMPUTERS AND CONSTRUCTION

As it turns out, the energy crisis that extended into 1974 helped the blanket industry, despite the mill's own rising costs of gas, propane and electricity. As the government beseeched Americans to lower the temperatures in their homes, consumers needed warmer clothes and blankets. Bob wrote:

> *Our line of woolen blankets has been a beneficiary of this developing situation since the natural fiber of wool is warmer and requires no energy to produce. Synthetic fibers of nylon, polyester, and acrylic are all derived from petro-chemicals and are, consequently, rising sharply in price although still less than half the cost of wool. These synthetic fibers lack the aesthetic and insulating properties of wool, and most of them burn very readily, posing the hazard of fire.*

In light of this comment, it's ironic that the *woolen* mill had five fires, the third of which burned the entire business to the ground.

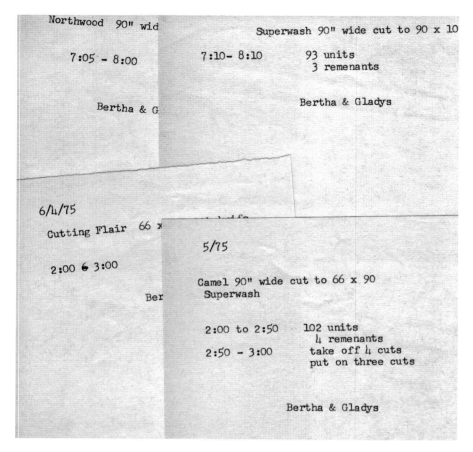

Northwood   90" wid

7:05 - 8:00

Bertha & G.

Superwash 90" wide cut to 90 x 10

7:10- 8:10   93 units
                  3 remenants

Bertha & Gladys

6/4/75

Cutting Flair   66 x

2:00 & 3:00

Ber

5/75

Camel 90" wide cut to 66 x 90
Superwash

2:00 to 2:50   102 units
                  4 remenants
2:50 - 3:00   take off 4 cuts
                  put on three cuts

Bertha & Gladys

These 1975 production notes are from employee team Bertha and Gladys. *Faribault Woolen Mill Archives.*

The Johnson family lost one of its members in 1975. Bob Johnson passed away, after retiring the year before, hindered by illness, a month after his wife.

The year the United States celebrated its bicentennial, the mill opted to add office space and a computer. Over one thousand square feet of space and three executive offices extended the narrow northeast corner. The computer arrived, and Bob Klemer wrote, "[A]fter many frustrating months of wrestling with programming problems, we were gradually able to reap some benefits from it, and it became a valuable addition to our office operations with many office functions and records now computerized. A larger and faster IBM computer was installed in 1980." Today, of course, Bob could have fit a *smaller* and faster computer in his suit pocket.

Also in the 1970s, the mill bought two more Duesberg-Bosson spinning frames, two stainless steel washers and a heat-exchange system that recycled heat from other processes. In 1979, it added a warehouse totaling 8,000 square feet; this addition made the mill an impressive 206,000 square feet. The registration form for the National Register of Historic Places lists the interior features, including "timber-framed [sections] with exposed brick walls…steel framing and exposed brick, concrete-block, or corrugated-metal walls…concrete [and wood] floors…exposed floor joists…bead-board ceilings…carpet, gypsum-board walls, and suspended acoustic-tile ceilings."

On a tour deep in the heart of the original mill, Dana Kielmeyer, an employee at the mill for over thirty-five years, showed me where old doors once closed, thresholds once extended, bricked windows once opened and roofline beams crossed so much shorter than the building now. It is a masterpiece of jigsaw.

THE LAST KLEMER PRESIDENT

Before he retired and was appointed chairman of the board of directors, Bob Klemer testified in yet another legislative hearing, this time about import duties. The Faribault Woolen Mill "initiated and promoted legislation in 1977 which eliminated import duties on coarser types of wool not produced in the U.S. These are principally the beautiful wools of New Zealand, which are so suitable for blankets." The legislation again passed.

Bob reasoned in his second history addendum that he felt the mill continued to succeed because so many other mills were closing. "During and immediately after World War II, there were at least 25 United States mills producing woolen blankets, several of them with very strong brand names such as St. Mary's, North Star, and Kenwood." Those brands were either absorbed into other companies or disappeared altogether. The Faribault Woolen Mill even stipulated contracts with the Lebanon Woolen Mills in Tennessee, a former woolen mill that had switched to acrylic.

Bob detailed the demise of the woolen mill more clearly:

> The end of World War II was quickly followed with the introduction of man-made fibers, principally nylon, acrylic and polyester. Many mills were quick to adopt these, since they could produce a lower priced product without the wide variation in market prices typical of the natural fibers, wool and

cotton. Many of the smaller Midwest woolen mills found it impossible to compete with the giant textile plants in the East and especially Southeast and were forced to liquidate. Recent years have seen a return of interest in the natural fibers due to their superior aesthetic qualities and a more affluent society willing to pay a higher price for a product with better appearance and hand.

Faribault adopted and converted part of their production to acrylic fiber about 1950, but continued to feature and promote all wools and 60% wool, 40% acrylic blends. This decision proved to be the right one since Faribault continued to prosper by meeting the increasing demand for better quality merchandise.

The numbers stood behind this rationale: the mill used 1 million pounds of fiber in 1972 compared to 1,500,000 seven years later; the total units sold went from 371,000 in 1972 to 1,100,000 in 1979; and the total sales went from $3,200,000 in 1972 to $10,900,000 in 1980.

When as many as eight Midwest woolen mills liquidated, the Faribault Woolen Mill bought some equipment to replace its slower and antiquated machines. Other equipment was also bought from mills in the East. Bottom line: efficiency and quality.

```
1975
TO:   ALL FOREMEN                                      Wool  118,013  2785  120798  2.3
FROM: Dick Klemer                                      Blend  40,179   848   41,027  2.1
                            PERCENT OF SECONDS CHART   Robes 378,197  3639  381,836  09
Please mark your chart as follows:
                                                              536,389  7,272  543,661  1.3
WEEK ENDING

Total seconds -        Wool -        Blend -        Robes -
% Seconds

1.  Stain               1982     27.25 %   10.  Unnapped           589    8.09 %
2.  Defective Selvage    322      4.42 %   11.  Serged Selvage     305    4.19 %
3.  Color Run-Streaked   499      6.86 %   12.  Defective Fringe   327    4.49 %
4.  Hole                 462      6.35 %   13.  Lint               227    3.12 %
5.  Light Places         143      1.97 %   14.  Short              119    1.63 %
6.  Grease Stain or       84      1.15 %   15.  Narrow              56    0.77 %
    Grease Selvage                         16.  Uneven Length      111    1.52 %
7.  Wrinkled               4      0.05 %   17.  Overnapped          33    0.45 %
8.  Misweave             740     10.17 %   18.  Mixed Filling      343    4.72 %
9.  Off Pattern          306      4.20 %   19.  Bars               620    8.52 %
```

An important part of recordkeeping, this is a Percent of Seconds Chart from 1975. *Faribault Woolen Mill Archives.*

In 1979, 114 years after Carl carded wool in a wooden building with his horse, an appraisal stated that to replace the woolen mill's components at the Cannon River site would cost over $3.5 million. To insure the equipment and building was over $2.7 million. Impressive numbers to match an impressive history.

Bob Klemer passed the presidential torch to his younger brother, Dick, in 1977, the fifth family member in four generations to lead the Faribault Woolen Mill Company. Bob began his "Addendum II, History of Faribault Woolen Mill Company 1960–1980":

> *The past two decades have been the most favorable ones in the history of our firm. The rapidly rising sales and resultant profits have been unprecedented and have made possible a very substantial program of capital investments for expansion and modernization of machinery, equipment, and building. This growth has been very rewarding and satisfying for many of us who worked through many lean years of very limited sales and profits.*

Yet in the mix of the modernization, it was the artisan skill, the work ethic of the people and the loyalty to the Klemers and Johnsons that also kept the mill in business. Ann Bickel, Boyd Sartell's daughter and Walter's granddaughter, said in *Book of Memories*, "My life was surrounded by the presence of the Woolen Mill, and I am fiercely and deeply proud of my family's connection to the mill, the mill's contributions to the community, and its loyal employees."

STILL STRONG IN THE '80S

Though at least one slide presentation given by Charlie Champlin in the 1990s documented more of the mill's successes in the 1980s, nothing came close to Frank's and Bob's detailed accounts of the mill's history. That history and its two addendums ended with Bob's comparison of mills open from 1945 to 1987 and the mills still existing in May 1987. Forty-five mills ran their businesses in 1945, while seven remained in 1987: two felt mills, three yarn spinners and two weaving plants. The latter showed the most significant drop from thirty-eight.

An article in the *Minneapolis Star* in February 1981 announced the mill's move to sell cotton blankets, a first for the company. This shift meant that Faribo used all three major fibers: wool, cotton and synthetics. "There has been a sharp

Yarn from a warper machine veils a mill employee in 1981. *Warren Reynolds photo, Faribault Woolen Mill Archives.*

decline in the number of domestic woolen mills since the turn of the century, from 1,500 to four or five." But, the article stated, "Faribo indicated that it was keeping the bulk of its manufacturing in wool because its quality cannot be duplicated." Pete Johnson, Ed Johnson's grandson and the retail sales manager at the time, felt that "consumers today will invest in better quality blankets as a means of holding down energy costs and that energy awareness 'spin-off' advantage of Faribo."

According to one set of slide show notes, the company started "marketing themes" for retail stores in 1983. The "High Road" theme was for just that— the higher-end markets of boutiques and refined department stores. The "World Class" theme, also aptly named, showcased woolen goods with fibers from around the world. Unnamed, the theme later focused on "fashion and color." Way before online mega-sites, the direct-mail market with companies like L.L. Bean and Land's End helped the mill with its retail success. It must be noted, however, that those companies had their own labels, not Faribault Woolen Mill's, sewed on the goods.

In 1986, the mill decided to build a new retail store across the street and just to the north of the Cannon River bridge. This building also became an

Inventory Dec 23, 1986
CUTS IN GREASE

~ 80"	Trapper Reg — 10		~ 90"	Bean Plaid Red — 3	
~ 90"	Wool · Thermal Multi — 16		~ 66"	Bean Plaid Blue — 3	
~ 90"	Americana Reg — 1		~ 66"	Bean Plaid Blackwatch — 1	
~ 80"	United — 40		66"	Bean Plaid Red — 10	
~ 96"	Melbourne Reg — 47		(90"	Faribo Red "Odd Lot" — 2)	
(90"	Harvest Reg — 4)		~ 5/60	County Fair Nat — 22	
~ 5/60	Merino Solid — 36 ?		~ 66"	Bean Plaid Wht — 10	
~ 72	Frontier Reg — 2		(50/70	Valencia — 3)	
~ 96"	W/SEF — 3		~ 5/60"	Wool · Throw — 23	
~ 90"	Trapper Reg — 15		~ 90"	Bean Plaid Wht — 9	
~ 90"	Americana Spec — 30		~ 5/60	Heather Wht — 14	
~ 90"	Trapper Reg w/S — 3		~ 5/60	Heather Blue — 3	
~ 90"	Satellite Reg — 59		~ 5/60	Mesa Wht — 3	
(90"	Nat Talent Reg —)				
~ 90"	Wool · Thermal — 96				
(90"	Nat Talent Spec — 280)				
~ 60"	Acrylic Solid — 14				
~ 66"	Trapper Reg — 9				

Above: An inventory for "cuts in grease," or raw, unprocessed woven goods, including L.L. Bean and airline products from December 1986. *Faribault Woolen Mill Archives.*

Right: A written memo request from October 1986 before the era of e-mail. *Faribault Woolen Mill Archives.*

memo   *Faribo*

Carol J. Johnson

to *Elmer*   date *10-15-86*

What are the Chances of getting 16,000 or 22,500 Merino Wool Scarves in gray w/1-color monogram delivered by January 2nd, 1987?

I need your answer by 1:30 if possible. Thanks.

Carol

20,000 ———

SCARF GIFT BOX ———

DESTINATION — ST. LOUIS, Mo., or CHICAGO, IL.

Faribault Woolen Mill Company
P.O. Box 369 Faribault, Minnesota 55021
(507) 334-6444

extra warehouse, the art department and photo studio and the embroidery and monogramming department. The mill once had a "Baby Hearts Crib Blanket" program, as well as a wedding throw program, that had monogram options on postcards for customers to mail in, but neither of those exists today. Leftover postcards have become part of the mill's history on the archive shelves.

More upkeep: the south dam closest to the mill received a new concrete surface in 1988.

The mill acquired a company called The Three Weavers in Houston, Texas, in 1989. Tom Klemer moved to the Lone Star State to be the general manager at the plant. Weavers signed each individual product, which made the merchandise unique. Tom stayed for three years before moving back home to Faribault to accept additional responsibilities, while remaining the general manager at The Three Weavers. Because the plant wasn't producing strong sales, it was sold to the plant manager a few years later. Weak sales snagged at what would come for the mill in the next decade.

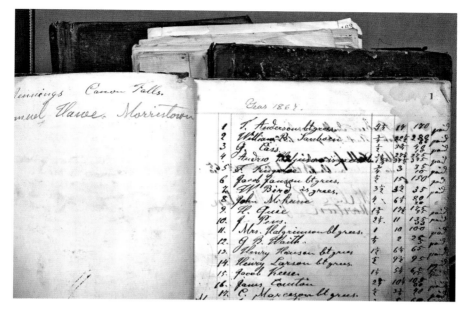

Carl Klemer's daybooks dated 1867–93, open to the first page of his 1867 daybook. *Photo by author, University Archives at Minnesota State University–Mankato.*

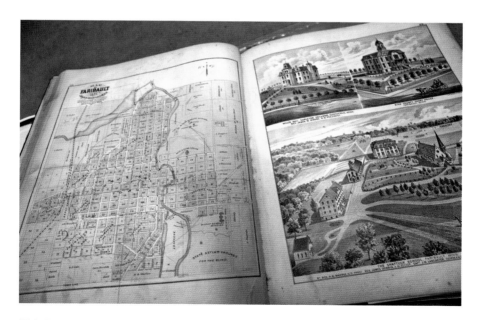

This Faribault map and illustrations are from the *Illustrated Historical Atlas of the State of Minnesota 1874. Photo by Jillian Raye Photography, Faribault Woolen Mill Archives.*

A 1917 olive drab (**OD**) military blanket used in France by an army soldier during World War I. *Photo by author, Faribault Woolen Mill Archives.*

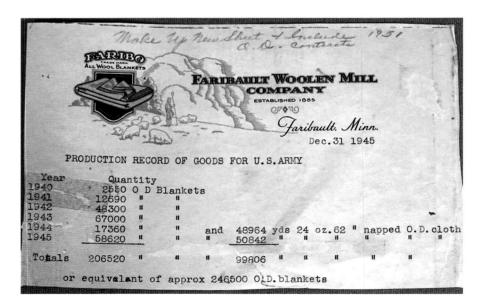

The record of goods made for the U.S. Army during World War II. *Photo by author, University Archives at Minnesota State University–Mankato.*

A washed wool ad showcased the durability of the mill's blankets, circa 1950s. *Photo by Jillian Raye Photography, Faribault Woolen Mill Archives.*

Arguably one of its most famous products, the Pak-a-Robe appeared in national magazines circa 1950s. *Faribault Woolen Mill Archives.*

a gift
of quality
and
beauty

Faribo

BLANKETS

. . . a reflection of your good
taste and thoughtfulness . . .
always warmly received and long-
enjoyed by even your most dis-
tinguished business associates . .
a gift that brings pleasure to all
who receive it.

100% Pure Wool
Individually Packaged
in Attractive Gift Box

Individual Mailing Service — 30c per mailing plus
postage. Individual shipping weight approximately
6-7 lbs. TERMS: Net F.O.B. Factory in Minnesota.
50c handling charge on shipments of less than 6.

EFFECTIVE 3-1-56

Form No. 58-B

PRINCETON
667-C-1—Size .66x90
2-11   12-24
$13.00 $12.00
25-49   50 & Over
$11.15 $10.40

667-B-3—Size 72x90
2-11   12-24
$14.00 $12.95
25-49   50 & Over
$12.00 $11.20

667-D-1—Size 80x90
2-11   12-24
$16.00 $14.75
25-49   50 & Over
$13.70 $12.80

BRADFORD
667-B-5—Size 72x90
2-11   12-29
$20.00 $18.45
25-49   50 & Over
$17.15 $16.00

COLORS:
Peacock Blue
Arctic White
Carnation Pink
Sahara Beige
Citron Yellow
Mint Green

Left: An ad dated 1956
for business gifts. Each
blanket cost twenty
dollars or less. *Faribault
Woolen Mill Archives.*

Below: This 1958–60
sewing and wrapping
spreadsheet is one
example of the mill's
extensive recordkeeping.
*Photo by Jillian Raye
Photography, Faribault
Woolen Mill Archives.*

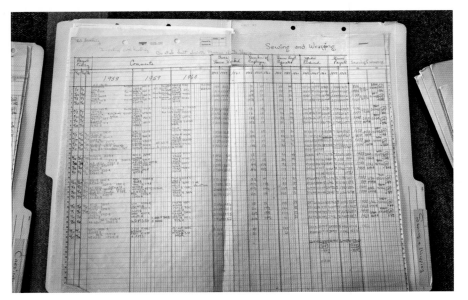

A full-color ad for blankets and sports robes, circa 1964. *Photo by author, Faribault Woolen Mill Archives.*

This ad showcases more variety in the mill's products: a robe, a throw and a blanket, circa 1960s. *Photo by author, Faribault Woolen Mill Archives.*

This aerial view circa the mid-1960s was taken before more square footage was added in 1972. *Photo by author, Faribault Woolen Mill Archives.*

In a meeting room, this burned beam visible above the fire truck photograph is a reminder of a minor 1960s fire. *Photo by Jillian Raye Photography.*

Above: In 1967, a gentleman returned his blanket with a letter, praising the 1930 gift and sharing its story. *Photo by author, Faribault Woolen Mill Archives.*

Right: An advertisement touting a blanket as the perfect use for a picnic, circa 1970s. *Faribault Woolen Mill Archives.*

Just-dyed wool before it's dried twice. Next at the picking house, dander and debris are removed before the wool is carded. *Photo by Jillian Raye Photography.*

One of the nine Davis & Furber carding machines. An employee painted this one. *Photo by Jillian Raye Photography.*

Carding machine #6 with its chalkboard, used for decades, states specifics about the wool being carded at the time. *Photo by Jillian Raye Photography.*

Cones with colored yarn await use. The warper is in the background. *Photo by Jillian Raye Photography.*

A cylindric warp beam, this one at the end of a run, feeds the loom. *Photo by author.*

A pattern machine for dobby looms; only one employee regularly programs it. Time will tell if/when and how it's replaced. *Photo by Jillian Raye Photography.*

A weave pattern punch card for dobby looms. Four of the twelve looms use it for perpendicular or ninety-degree patterns. *Photo by Jillian Raye Photography.*

Yellow harness cords on the jacquard loom allow circular or diagonal patterns to be woven into fabric. *Photo by Jillian Raye Photography.*

The yellow cords control the harness, lifting and lowering the warp yarn to weave this striped blanket. *Photo by Jillian Raye Photography.*

A loom weaves a black blanket with red and teal stripes. *Photo by Jillian Raye Photography.*

A loom cuts the middle of the fabric to make smaller throws. *Photo by Jillian Raye Photography.*

The 1776 Flag Wool Throw, first produced in 2012, on the napper. *Photo by Jillian Raye Photography.*

Two mill employees cut yardage into individual blankets. This same process has been documented in photos for generations. *Photo by Jillian Raye Photography.*

These throws and scarves decorate the main conference room, but the display is always changing. *Photo by Jillian Raye Photography.*

The retail store displays bold colors and soft earth tones in the mill's products. *Photo by Jillian Raye Photography.*

The mill collection includes University of Minnesota goods. *Photo by Jillian Raye Photography.*

The mill honors one of Minnesota's iconic sites, the Boundary Waters Canoe Area Wilderness (BWCAW), in this store display. *Photo by Jillian Raye Photography.*

The new wearables and factory seconds—blankets, throws and scarves with minor and often unseen imperfections—in the mill store. *Photo by Jillian Raye Photography.*

Chapter 6

UNRAVELING

Heritage Days is Faribault's signature small-town celebration. It's what Dam Days is to Morristown, the Defeat of Jesse James Day is to Northfield, the Macy's Thanksgiving Day Parade is to New York City. In the weeklong celebration's eighth year in 1990, the Faribault Woolen Mill decided to create the world's largest blanket to celebrate the mill's 125 years.

On June 23, 1990, thirty-six volunteers laid out 420 of the 1,230 donated blankets and sewed them together at Bruce Smith Field, where Faribault High School and Bethlehem Academy football teams still play. In Pauline Schreiber's *Faribault Daily News* article the day before, Charlie Champlin, the marketing director, said they received about three times the number of blankets they had hoped for. The blanket ended up laying 85 feet wide by 185 feet long, or 15,725 square feet. At the time, this size was 5,000 feet larger than the record holder in *The Guinness Book of World Records*. After the display ended later in the day, volunteers separated the blankets and gave them to the Salvation Army.

In *Book of Memories*, Paul Schell added more to the largest blanket story:

After posing employees and visiting dignitaries in front of the World's Largest Blanket, I sprinted up the football stadium bleachers to climb the ladder leading to the roof of the announcer's booth. As I was nearing the top of the ladder, it began to pull free of the building. The ladder and I teetered for what seemed like a lifetime 40 feet over the stadium parking lot. I pressed myself into the ladder and slowly tipped forward. I don't

Volunteers and friends gather at Bruce Smith Field with the largest blanket on June 23, 1990, to celebrate 125 years. *Faribault Woolen Mill Archives.*

remember the photo shoot that followed; all I could think of was how amusing my death would have been to everyone watching.

In 1991, a controversy was averted, thanks to the mill, when the Minnesota Twins baseball team won the World Series. Four years before when the Twins won and held victory parades in the downtowns of Minneapolis and St. Paul, the players wore mink coats. Voices of dissent rang loud. The parade organizer, a friend of President Pete Johnson's, contacted the mill the morning of the parade, needing two hundred blankets by that afternoon. Johnson and Scott Markman, specialty sales manager, drove the red plaid blankets to the Cities. The blankets were worn by the players and then donated to the Minnesota Twins Community Fund, a charity affiliated with a children's shelter.

Another sporting event helped promote the mill. The *Counselor*, a periodical for marketing professionals, reported that the mill was asked to donate a product to the five thousand volunteers when the Super Bowl was held in Minneapolis in 1992. The company opted to make scarves that were embroidered with the Super Bowl XXVI logo, as well as Faribo's logo with its three spindles. Bright red, the scarves reflected the theme of the game: "Minnesota, This Is the Hottest Time of the Year." Markman spoke about this specialty item for these volunteers. Besides being practical, "it gave them something to keep after the weekend as a souvenir and a gift."

In the summer of 1993, Bob passed away at age eighty-two, joining his family in the Klemer plot near Carl, his great-grandfather. Perhaps, now knowing the unraveling that was in store for the mill, it was better for Bob to be resting peacefully in the cemetery.

Charlie Champlin, a twenty-eight-year veteran, wrote in *Book of Memories*:

> *We enjoyed a continual pattern of sales growth from the early '70s until the early '90s. We began to lose ground in the early 1990s to substitute product and cheaper imports. It was a slow and subtle change, but it really hit home when we lost the United Airlines account in 1994. United kept the looms running because of the sheer volume they represented. Losing United meant multiple shifts were no longer possible and overhead costs began to climb.*

The Faribault Woolen Mill Company wasn't the only mill languishing. More textile weaving companies left for overseas; several closed. In an August 1997 article in *Monthly Labor Review*, Mark Mittelhauser wrote, "Between 1973 and 1996, nearly a million jobs were lost in the textile and apparel industries combined—a decline of nearly 40 percent."

OUTSIDE INVESTORS

In 1997, the Klemer family and the mill management team felt the company was headed for trouble. The team—including Tom, brother Dave Klemer and third-generation Pete Johnson—decided to bring in an outside investor group. Peter Lytle and Bill Haskamp stepped in to run the company; they held a majority interest, while the Klemers and Johnsons held a minority interest.

Lytle asked Michael Harris, or the "rainmaker," to find investors in order to create a "bricks and clicks strategy," according to public federal documents. The bricks would stay in Faribault, of course, while the clicks would mean opening up "an e-commerce site" to sell the mill's products. At the time, no one at the mill knew who Harris was, perhaps other than as an investor name, but he claimed, "I was asked to find investors to take over and revive the company. And I was pretty good at that back then and it was easier back then." Harris said, "That's how I got my ownership, my .22 percent."

Carl's great-great-grandsons, Dave and Tom Klemer. *Photo by Jillian Raye Photography, Faribault Woolen Mill Archives.*

The *Faribault Daily News* published a story on April 29, 1998, that read, "All 156 workers will be retained, Lytle said, and plans call for employment to at least double in two years." The management team included Chief Operations Officer Bill Haskamp, President Charlie Champlin, Co-Vice-President Tom Klemer, Co-Vice-President David Klemer and President Brenda Borwege of Faribo Woolens Inc., the company under the mill that managed stores in Faribault and Red Wing, Minnesota. Lytle also spoke of trying to find a new female CEO "because most buyers are women." Talks were underway to potentially acquire other mills, while the Faribault mill would possibly be doubled in size over the next two to three years. The Faribault Woolen Mill's owners "could have made a lot more money if they'd chosen to sell to someone on the outside," Lytle said. "They've had a lot of offers over the years, but they didn't want to sell without assurances that it was going to continue on."

Tom Klemer said that sometime in the early 1990s, a company called Pillowtek offered to buy the Faribault Woolen Mill. It would have meant a multimillion-dollar deal for the family, and his dad, Dick, encouraged Tom to consider it. But, Tom said, he believed Pillowtek would have closed down the mill. (According to its website, Pillowtek succumbed to bankruptcy in 2004 and was bought by another unnamed company and is in business today.) Tom didn't want to sell. He felt he was young enough to keep the mill business going, and he honestly believed he'd retire someday from the Faribault company. For Tom, there was no negotiation.

"Not only no, but hell no," Tom said.

In hindsight, he admitted, he should have said yes because he could have turned around and bought everything back when Pillowtek sold it.

Eventually, the name of the new business with Lytle, Haskamp, Harris and others became North American Heritage Brands. In Peter Lytle's obituary just over ten years later, he was listed as the CEO of this new company, not of the Faribault Woolen Mill. It was North American Heritage Brands that bought a cotton mill called Bates of Maine and merged with Dakotah Inc., a company based in South Dakota that made home furnishings. The latter deal "is expected to provide cost savings of $2 million to $3 million in the first year by combining design, product development, marketing, procurement and administrative efforts," reported a September 1998 *Star Tribune* article.

By mid-September 1998, it was announced that Warren Malkerson, an L.L. Bean executive, would become the CEO of the Faribault Woolen Mill and Dakotah Inc. on October 15. Champlin remained president, and Lytle remained chairman of the board. In December 1998, *Star Tribune* reporter Susan E. Peterson wrote that Malkerson said the "Bates sales are expected to nearly double in 1999 and to double again within three years." In addition, Lytle added, "The plan is to create a family of strategic American brands that will bring economies of scale in advertising, marketing, sales and operations."

The plan, then, seemed to call for a multi-blended family that reached far from Faribault.

2K

In Cynthia Elyce Rubin's *Fiberarts* article dated March/April 2000, CEO Malkerson spoke of new mill collections "that reflect America's history and diversity." A buffalo rancher in South Dakota inspired the jacquard-woven throws collection "made of a unique blend of buffalo fibers and wool, with designs inspired by Native American legends and the Southwest petroglyphs." Another collection celebrated the bicentennial of the Lewis and Clark expedition with its embroidered throws, "reflecting life on the trail." In addition, "Various tribal-inspired blankets were being made into coats and jackets for the first time, thereby combining Faribault's old-fashioned craftsmanship and tradition with high fashion." Rubin wrote, "[W]ith a recent infusion of new capital, Faribault is well poised for the 21st century."

Business was going well, at least on paper.

By the time Rubin's article was in print, however, Malkerson was gone, replaced by Marshall Masko, who "brings to North American Heritage more than 20 years marketing and management experience at some of the best-known brand franchises in America," declared a March 2000 article in *Home Textiles Today*.

Tom Klemer said, "I butted my head" with both Masko and another executive; they didn't agree on how the mill was being run. Tom felt the management team was "pouring a lot of money into dot coms, and they weren't addressing the issues that needed to be addressed like [new owners] the Mootys have done, whether it be infrastructure, equipment, spare parts, employees, the bones." Tom was still working more than sixty hours a week, and he was still experiencing frustration and stress. "Now I was a minority owner, and they weren't interested in listening to me and what I had to say about our clients, our industry, our employees, things of that nature." Tom sought other employment as the management steadily decreased his responsibilities.

Depending on whom you ask, Tom resigned/retired/was let go in the fall of 2000. Dave Klemer and Pete Johnson resigned/retired/were let go in early 2001.

In Tom's words:

> *That's probably the second most…well, first or second most heartbreaking moment of my life was having to leave. The first one was making the decision to bring in outside investors because it had always been a family-owned company. But I had to make that decision, you know, am I saving a legacy that's going to die and keep it in the family, or do I do the greater good to save the company and the employees and everything else? In 1997, about thirteen, fourteen years out of college, I had to start making some tough decisions. Well, with Pete and others, but…a lot of it was…That was the probably the hardest time of my life.*

According to federal documents, about the time the Klemers and Johnsons lost the family business, Lytle asked Harris to go to the mill. During this visit, the mill's controller pulled Harris aside when "Peter [Lytle] didn't want to hear about it" and said the financial picture was quite grim. Harris decided it was time for him to actually be part of the mill versus just a shareholder, when he "saved it again." He continued: "[A]ll these people were going to lose their jobs because nobody wanted this business, nobody." After he heard the new mortgage lender was persuading the management to liquidate, Harris said, "I raised the money to take care of the people and keep the woolen mill and the cotton mill up and alive."

By 2001, the mill was $4 million in the black but $12 million in the red. Harris found money to invest in the mill from local funds, as well as from the richest man in Poland, who knew firsthand what was happening to woolen mills in Poland and Western Europe. Both the Bates Mill and the Internet site were shut down while funds from a private foundation allowed the Faribault Woolen Mill to buy a South Carolina mill. According to the *Minneapolis Star Tribune*, as soon as Harris moved into his executive positions, Rice County Sheriff Cook "showed up [at the mill] regularly to serve 27 judgments—the result of commercial disputes with the company's former management."

LONG-RANGE PLAN

In July 2002, Harris, the CEO of the Faribault Woolen Mill, wrote a "Long-Range Plan." The thick presentation was placed in a white binder that can be found in the mill's archives. In the "Company Overview: History" section, Harris wrote, "During the 1990s, the two founding families started to have differing opinions on how the mill should be run. One family cashed out, the other stayed on to run the company. In 1998, the remaining family was forced to sell the company." Further, "As of early 2001 when Mr. Harris took over as Chairman, President & CEO, all board members and senior management has been replaced."

Harris introduced the holding company called North American Heritage Brands, Inc. Later in the presentation, it stated that Harris was appointed chairman, president and CEO of that holding company, not the Faribault Woolen Mill.

In the "Employees" section, Harris complimented the more than one hundred "skilled artisan employees" and wrote, "It is this base of intellectual knowledge of wool and woolen products that will be so important when volume, demand and new products grow dramatically."

Harris highlighted the industry, specified buyers and included a wish list of thirty-three future customers. A flow chart named his sales and marketing staff; an additional chart listed all of his key personnel. On the graph for sales projections, 2003 had almost $23 million listed, while 2006 more than tripled at almost $77 million.

The opinion of today's management about that last figure? It's fiction.

In the "Financial Review" section, Harris wrote:

> *2001 was a year of tremendous change for our companies. Unfortunate economic and industry situations created an environment where liquidation seemed eminent. Mike Harris, one of the minority shareholders, was informed of the situation in January. He did an evaluation of the current position and asked the other shareholders for an opportunity to save the company and the jobs of over 100 employees of the oldest company in Minnesota. Mike took over in February and asked for the resignation of almost all management.*
>
> *We have taken the position to get all the "sins" behind and go forward on firm and accountable ground. The corporate structure is as follows: North American Heritage Brands, Inc. (NAHB) is the parent company of three wholly owned subsidiaries, Faribault Woolen Mill Company (FWMC), e-Bedroom, and Globaltex dba Bates of Maine. FWMC is the manufacturing company and is the parent company of one wholly subsidiary, Faribo Woolens Inc. (FWI). FWI is our retail outlet store.*

BAD NEWS, GOOD NEWS

Opposite the optimism of Harris's plan, the Faribault Woolen Mill laid off three employees in October 2002. "All the workers will be called back as soon as we find the capital to buy additional wool," Harris said in a *Faribault Daily News* article by Pauline Schreiber. "Our outlook is better than it's ever been. Temporary layoffs in production, however, will keep occurring because of our capital restraints."

On the flip side, in mid-November 2004, Schreiber wrote an article about a new product that the Faribault Woolen Mill had been producing for about a year. Working with a Cargill Dow partnership, the mill developed a new fiber from corn called Ingeo. Dennis Melchert, who at the time was chief operations officer at the mill, told me that he was "the dreamer" of the idea after attending the Frankfurt Textile Show, wanting to find a replacement for acrylic. In the article, Melchert said, "The Ingeo fiber can be spun into yarn either by itself or blended with wool." These biodegradable blankets "are flame retardant, wick moisture away from the body like wool, and are very soft to the touch," Harris said. It even won the Governor's Award for Environmental Excellence in 2004 and was marketed by John Deere and other agricultural businesses.

Decidedly, not everyone was on board. Marshall Field's and other stores showed little warmth toward the product. Harris admitted in Schreiber's article that the Ingeo blanket hadn't generated profits, but "I expect it to be soon." Melchert told me that it was an excellent product, but the process got more complicated with a larger volume versus being made in a prototype factory. Veteran employee Mary Boudreau, after rolling her eyes when I mentioned the fiber, retorted, "It should've stayed in the cornfield."

The mill produced the Ingeo blankets for about three years.

The end of 2004 featured a collaboration of two of the oldest establishments in Faribault: the woolen mill and Shattuck–St. Mary's. The former created a merino wool blanket for the school in its colors, embroidered with the iconic logo of the outline of the buildings, sixty-four by eighty inches, perfect for either outdoor or indoor use. The manager of the school's store was quoted in the *Faribault Daily News*: "People have the idea wool is scratchy, but the new process for making wool blankets makes it very soft."

For about five years, the press seemed to stay relatively quiet about the mill. Inside, however, the mill unraveled.

CHAPTER 7

FATE LOCKED THE
MILL'S DOOR

Type "layoffs" in the search bar of the *Faribault Daily News* website, and you will see article after article from southern Minnesota reporting cutbacks: in 2007, the Faribault School District; in 2008, the City of Northfield, Allina Clinic and the Faribault Court System. In 2009, McNeilus Trucking and Manufacturing in Dodge Center; Brown Printing in Waseca; Viracon, Truth Hardware and SPX in Owatonna; and McQuay International (now Daikin Global) in both Owatonna and Faribault.

The Faribault Woolen Mill also began 2009 in turmoil. Federal documents show that on February 11, 2009, the Faribault Woolen Mill Company applied for a new deposit business account. Three people, including Harris, were listed as authorized signers. Annual gross sales were noted at $8 million; this figure came from December 30, 2007. For the industry, the application stated, "wood/plastic/glass/chemical manufacturing"—everything the woolen mill was not.

The March 7, 2009 *Faribault Daily News* headline online read, "Shaken, but Not Broken: Faribault Mills CEO Says Company Will Stay the Course." Harris asserted, "It's a difficult time for any business. Everybody is going through difficult times." Further, "While I'd like to think that I've fixed everything, I haven't quite fixed everything. Money's tight." Yet according to the business information site Hoovers.com, the newspaper reported, the mill recorded sales of $25 million in 2008.

The article also quoted a three-month employee, saying she and other employees had trouble cashing their paychecks. "Anna," an employee I interviewed who had worked at the mill about fifteen years when it closed, said the paychecks at the end were always bouncing. When the employees were asked to do a military blanket order, Anna said, no one was paid for that job.

Mary Boudreau, an employee of almost fifty-five years at that time, told me, "I don't know how long some of them didn't get paid for how many weeks. I always made sure I got mine because I went right back up to him [Harris] if my check didn't go through. They'd say, 'I'll call the bank, and you go right back down there.'"

"Did you have to do that often?" I asked.

"A few times I did, yes," Boudreau said.

In the March *Faribault Daily News* article, Harris said that problem was taken care of. Most importantly, he contended:

> *I'm firmly 100 percent, 120 percent, 150 percent committed to keeping the mill and the company open…We're the finest blanket company in the world and we plan on honoring that tradition. I'm doing everything in my power to make sure the company stays in Faribault another 140 years.*

On Monday, just two days later, the mill laid off twenty employees, or 25 percent of its workforce.

In that article, reporter Corey Butler wrote that Harris said, "Closing the mill is not an option." Further, "It's almost an impossibility," Harris said. "If I felt there was doom and gloom, I wouldn't be here. I'm very confident that we'll be here tomorrow and the next day and the next day and the next day for the next 140 years." Even after the paycheck cashing woes and laying off employees, Harris still believed he could save the mill.

Meanwhile, federal documents showed that Harris, as well as all of the employees, received a letter from HealthPartners dated February 28, 2009, that "your employer is now delinquent with their premium payment. We will cancel your policy in 30 days retroactive to January 31, 2009." However, "If your employer pays all past due premiums within the 30-day period, your coverage will continue without a break in service."

The policy was cancelled.

BILLS

According to an April *Faribault Daily News* article titled "CEO: Woolen Mills 'Within Days' of Closure," Harris sent an e-mail to the Faribault City

Council. He asked for absolution, to not be held responsible for the water bill, which was $140,000. Without assistance, the doors would be locked "within days." The article reported that "the company has a 'huge backlog' of orders and that he has already leveraged $1 million of his personal assets to keep the company afloat." Harris claimed if the mill closed, his family would suffer, and he'd lose his home.

The decision was difficult to make for the Faribault City Council. It had to weigh several factors—the water bill revenue for the city, the financial and emotional cost of losing jobs, the potential loss of the oldest private company in the state. In May, the council made a decision six to one in favor of Harris. One supporting member, council member Carol King, said in a *Faribault Daily News* article, "The woolen mills are very dear to my heart…If they're even going to have a chance, we're going to have to go forward with this." Council member Steve Underdahl, however, felt apprehensive that the arrangement would open the door for future businesses experiencing financial problems and voted against the arrangement. In the deal with Harris, $121,252 of the bill would be forgiven as long as he agreed to a five-year, interest-free payment. The city also wanted the mill to pay about $43,000 in water bills, charged since the beginning of 2009, within forty-five days. It also stipulated that the city could "assess the sum of the outstanding debt against the property owner again if the company defaults or is sold." The mill in South Carolina was closed, and the retail store emptied the space of its woolen goods, departments and storage.

In filed federal documents, a shareholder report from May 23, 2009, lists sixty-five names of individuals and organizations with stock in the company. Harris owned 25.22 percent of the mill. The Schwan Foundation owned 43.05 percent. Collectively, the Klemers owned less than 1 percent, while Pete Johnson owned .55 percent.

On June 12, 2009, the company had a loan balance with the Economic Development Administration of close to $300,000, and rent hadn't been paid to FWF Fund One, the landowners, since November 2008.

On July 14, 2009, the *Faribault Daily News* posted a story online with the title "Woolen Mill Future Remains Unclear."

The end had come.

Reporter Kay Fate wrote:

> *Depending on who you talk to, the Woolen Mills has closed after 144 years in business. "I know it's been stressful for the last week or so," Faribault Mayor John Jasinski said Tuesday. Still, no official word has come down.*

"The hope of the board is to be able to continue to provide a quality place to work and a quality product," said Mark Michel, an outside independent contractor of the Woolen Mills. "The company has stopped operations because it needs working capital," he said. "There have been a number of efforts by a lot of well-intentioned people. Our issue is financial." Officials with the Schwan Foundation, the senior creditor in the business, did not immediately return phone calls seeking comment. A trip to the facility on Tuesday found the parking lot empty, and one employee in the makeshift retail store, now housed within the mill itself. That employee refused to speak publicly on the situation but agreed that the facility had closed. Not true, says former CEO Michael Harris. "To my knowledge, it's not closed; it's just not in operational format," he said Tuesday by phone. When asked to explain, Harris said that the plant "is just not operating today or tomorrow." He refused to comment further.

When I asked Dennis Melchert if he was the last person to lock the doors, he said he locked the warehouse but not the office space.

"Then who locked the office door when everyone left?"

"I never left," Melchert said. He kept coming back to the mill periodically to make sure the equipment still functioned.

"So who locked the door for the last time that day in 2009?"

He thought for a moment.

"Fate," Melchert said. "Fate locked the door that last day."

CHAPTER 8

MEMORIES, THE MOOTYS AND A LAWSUIT

It was as if the mill had been taken for granted. After all, despite its ups and downs, it had survived fires and firings. But to actually close? It must have felt agonizing to those who drove by the mill every day, seeing the empty parking lots, knowing the building had no more artisans—their friends and family—crafting quality woolen goods after almost a century and a half of prosperity.

Faribault Foods, which had a local beginning in Carl's day, decided to lease the empty woolen mill retail store across from the mill in December 2009. After a facelift, it opened in May 2010 as an office building. An editorial in the *Faribault Daily News* stated, "All good news for Faribault Foods and Faribault's tax base. An empty building does not help the city. But one that is repurposed and up and running does."

Then came news of the mill itself. A linen manufacturer out of Philadelphia called Paradise Pillow Inc. contacted the Faribault Economic Development Authority in July 2010. The *Faribault Daily News* reported that "the company wants to lease the woolen mill site from the current owners to deal with increased demand from growing numbers of government contracts." The president of Paradise noted that the company would keep the mill's name, and he also expressed interest in working with former employees. It was hard to imagine the empty building full of comforters, pillows and sheets instead of fine woolen goods, but the deal never transpired.

On September 23, 2010, as if the reservoir and Cannon River threw a tantrum because the building stood empty, floodwaters ravaged the mill.

The Straight River crested around fourteen and a half feet. The damage was so extensive in the state that President Obama approved Minnesota governor Tim Pawlenty's request for a federal disaster declaration. When the water receded, the mill rested on the riverbank empty and damaged.

MEMORIES

Jeff Jarvis, a City of Faribault employee who had relatives working at mills in the late 1800s/early 1900s, and LaVonne Brick, a former employee of the Faribault Woolen Mill, decided to sustain the mill with memories. They gave questionnaires to the mill staff and compiled their answers into *Book of Memories*. Some people answered with one or two words; others wrote paragraphs about their time at the company. Woolen Mill Coffee Hours in town were the time to share with others and reconnect with old friends.

One of the themes that resonates in the book is the idea of family. Ann Bickel, Boyd Sartell's daughter and Walter Klemer's granddaughter, summed it up this way: "My 'blanket memories' bounces from our house to the mill and back—they're sometimes hard to separate because the mill was really the fabric of my family and my youth." Many employees had relatives who had worked at the mill. Janelle Zitzmann, in fact, had five sisters who had also worked there.

Blood relatives weren't the only family mentioned. Doug Remmey, who was at the mill for twenty-nine and a half years, wrote, "My best memory was the camaraderie, the feeling that we were all family. There was a closeness that wouldn't be found in a larger company." Elmer Schultz, at the mill for forty-six years, wrote, "Most vivid memory is that of all of us being one large family—working together to produce high-quality products for thousands of people."

Longevity becomes apparent in *Book of Memories*, too: over fifty years of employment, forty-seven, forty-two, thirty-four, thirty, twenty-nine and a half—decades of dedication.

Other stories relate the humor, the pranks and the foolery. Georgy Caron remembered "the food fight at Millersburg and bringing a Faribo blanket to the waitress the next day as part of an apology." Laura Krenske recalled "when someone brought a fake snake to work and would hide it in a blanket that someone was working on." Dave Klemer wrote, "Cleaning out the dye kettle's waste tanks during the summer shutdown and having the foremen all coming down to see the youngest Klemer knee deep in stinking waste water." For Dennis Gregor's most humorous story, he wrote, "Wouldn't know where to start."

Pete Johnson wrote about his grandfather, Ed:

> *When Ed worked for North Star Woolen Mills, his brother Fred was also an employee of North Star. Fred's job was to buy wool and be involved in sales. When Ed moved to Faribault, he also got involved in sales and found his very own brother a formidable competitor. The brothers were always socially close, but when it came time for them to get out into the market for sales orders, they would not talk to each other. Neither knew if he was the first to make the sales calls or would be following his brother to pick up stray orders that the first brother missed.*

Though almost all the stories spoke of hard work, laughter, family and/or friendship, one employee who had been at the mill for nineteen years held nothing back: "I think it's a shame you have to be writing a Woolen Mills Memory Book. It is possible for the ego of management to betray loyal, hardworking people and it was those people who made the Woolen Mill what it was. So many bad decisions by management equals a Woolen Mills *Memory* Book." Another echoed his sentiments: "The Klemers valued their employees and that was apparent when you saw so many family members working at the mill for so many years. Unfortunately, value and loyalty had been lost over the years. If you don't value your employees, how can you expect loyalty?"

A March 2011 article in the *Faribault Daily News* stated that the Faribault mill closure even affected the Routt County Woolens in Steamboat Springs, Colorado. After only fourteen years, it was forced to sell its inventory because the Faribault mill would no longer be able to provide the woven wool to the Colorado company.

The dam kept spilling water from the reservoir into the Cannon River. The traffic kept driving past on Second Avenue Northwest. The mill stood noble but hushed.

TIMING AND TOURS

Paul Mooty, one of the cousins who ended up buying the mill, told the story of timing:

I almost didn't come down here…It was another Dennis. His son, Chris, was my fraternity brother and roommate in college, and I hadn't talked to Chris in twenty-some years, or twenty-five years, and he called me up one day and he said, "Hey, my dad would like to talk to you about something." I talked to Dennis, and he said, "Well, I'm looking at this mill, I've got this letter of intent." This was like Wednesday. "And it expires on Friday but wanted to know if you wanted to get involved." I just said no. I just said, "No, no, no." So I just ignored it. He sent me some e-mails that I kind of ignored. A few weeks later, I was dumping e-mails on my computer, and I saw Dennis's e-mail, and I opened it up. Wow, that's kind of interesting. So I said, "Can we still go down there? I know you lost your letter of intent, but can we go down and visit the mill?" And he said, "Well, I'll set something up with Dennis [Melchert].*" And that's the day I came down here. Had I deleted the e-mail, I wouldn't have done it. And had Dennis not been here to give that tour, had I just come in here and someone said, "Here's a set of keys, why don't you walk through the place and tell me what you think," I would've said, "I think you're nuts." But Dennis was here, and I went home, said to my wife, "It's kind of a messy place, but there's something special down there." That was because Dennis had the passion…he loved the place, and he conveyed that message. If* [Chris's dad] *Dennis hadn't called me and said, "Hey, would you like to look at the mill," I wouldn't have known about it, either.*

Paul also spoke of others, like his uncle John, whom he conversed with instead of his dad, who was in ill health at the time. Paul admired and respected his uncle. Even after John spoke to someone who portrayed the mill as grim, John told his nephew he should look into the mill a bit more.

On March 8, 2011, Paul took a tour of the deserted Faribault Woolen Mill. In the basement, the flood had marked up the walls—which were light blue because of the dye that had swirled with the water—up to an exit sign. Dust iced the equipment. There was no way it could be operable. But by the time Paul reached the top floor, he started changing his mind—Dennis's stories of the mill sang in his ears. Paul told his first cousin Charles "Chuck" Mooty, John's son, to take a tour as well. Chuck also went by himself that first time while Paul was out of town. Chuck, too, was wooed by its history and potential.

The two cousins returned to the mill in the beginning of April. Chuck turned to his cousin and said, "Paul, I think we can do this." The exact same thought had crossed their minds at the same time. By the end of April, the

First cousins Paul and Chuck Mooty bought the Faribault Woolen Mill in 2011. *Photo by Jillian Raye Photography.*

cousins had a letter of intent, which saved the already tagged equipment from being sold. The transaction moved quite fast, but the cousins felt quite sure about their decision. They knew what the mill had been and felt they knew what could make it flourish again. Jean Mooty, Paul's wife, pointed out, "When we first saw the mill…It hadn't been loved in a long time."

It wasn't until June 2011 that Faribault found out about the Mootys: Chuck, the former CEO of International Dairy Queen, and Paul, a lawyer who had recently managed a different business. Chuck planned to be the CEO and president, while Paul would be the CFO. *Faribault Daily News* reporter Joseph Lindberg wrote that Chuck "stressed the cooperative and family-oriented nature of the venture, stressing his desire to be an active ownership team." First, the cousins had to wait for the results of the hearing for FWF Fund One's $72,000 utility bills, paid down from more than $100,000. Second, the business needed renovation. Third, the mill needed employees back.

The first hurdle, the utility bill, was in the Mootys' favor—the city council voted to absolve the old debt. Lindberg wrote an article about the people who attended the meeting: "Support came from all parts of Faribault society, reflecting the deep roots and emotional connection the mill built with its residents over its [almost] 150-year history." Former mayor Dean Purdie commented, "They make such a high-quality product, and it's incredibly important to this community." Further:

> Several former employees turned out to support the assessment forgiveness. "When you say Faribault to people, the first thing they ask about is the mills," said Carla Craig. That theme kept creeping into the dialogue. Faribault's Chamber of Commerce President Kymn Anderson said the number one inquiry the chamber gets is still the woolen mill. "They want to know where to get blankets and how to take a tour," she said.

Despite the overwhelming support, an editorial in the local paper expressed disappointment. The concern was about other businesses asking to be excused from bills if this decision started a new standard, a repeat concern from when former CEO Harris asked to be pardoned from the mill's utility bill in 2009.

Still, the deal closed on June 30, 2011.

The second hurdle was finding funds to repair and renovate the mill. The Faribault Woolen Mill Company hired a historical consultant from Hess, Roise and Company in Minneapolis to complete the National Register of Historic Places registration form for the United States Department of the Interior, National Park Service. The form is dated December 30, 2011.

Under "Description," the consultant wrote:

> The mill retains good historic integrity and all seven aspects of integrity are present. The mill has integrity of location and setting. The company milled and produced woolen goods here since 1892. The area surrounding the mill remains much as it has been with the Cannon River and dams to the west and north; Second Avenue NW, a railroad spur, and a cannery to the east; and a residential neighborhood to the south and southwest. The building also has integrity of design, with its particular spatial arrangement dictated by the requirements of wool processing. Equipment was updated as technology changed and as the company's business grew. This led to a series of utilitarian additions, which are physical representations of the history of the company. The materials—brick, concrete block, and corrugated metal on the exterior and timber and steel framing on the interior—are typical of the eras that produced them and retain good integrity. The building materials are placed as they originally were showing integrity of workmanship in the construction. Together, these physical features, along with the building's continued use as a woolen mill, contribute to the property's integrity of feeling and association.

On February 13, 2012, the mill was notified that the application would be reviewed by the state. The meeting occurred at the end of March, and by June, the board informed the mill it would be added to the more than seventy other Rice County buildings on the National Register in ninety days. Besides the recognition, the designation meant the Mootys could apply for Legacy Amendment dollars and Historic Preservation Tax Credits.

They applied.

In July 2012, the Minnesota State Historic Preservation Office said it didn't see how the public would be able to take full advantage of the mill's repair, while the Faribault Heritage Preservation Commission disagreed. By September, the debate was over: the Minnesota Historical Society awarded the mill a $300,000 grant to help with the estimated $315,000 restoration. Two years later, the company applied for state and federal tax credits, which also helped with the mill's renovation.

The last but definitely not least hurdle in mid-2011: the workforce, the marrow of the mill. The phone calls, the home visits, the word of mouth began. Dana Kielmeyer, who started at the mill in 1979, said he knew something was going on when he saw two cars, then four cars and got eight phone calls. "It was meant to be," he said. "It was what I'd done for thirty-three years."

Paul and Chuck invited former employees to a meeting in the summer of 2011. Anna, a current employee, said about twenty of the original workforce sat around the conference room table with Paul and Chuck. The cousins asked the employees if they would be interested in returning to the mill in the beginning of August. After listening to the cousins, talking among themselves and speaking with Avinash Bhatnagar, the vice-president of mill operations, who told the former employees that "the new owners came in with good intentions," those around the table gave Paul and Chuck their names, addresses and phone numbers.

"I was looking for work," Anna said, "and I wasn't having much luck, and I thought, 'I'm all trained in. At least get my foot back in the door.' I thought, 'I'm going to do it, try it.' So that's why I did it."

"There must've been some sort of feeling, like, okay…" I started.

"What if this happens again?" Anna said.

"Yes, what if this happens again."

"There was, there was," Anna admitted. "But as time went on and on and on, we could see it was better, it was good, it was going to be okay."

When the employees returned in August 2011, everything was exactly how they had left it on that last day in 2009, except now there was an inch of dust on everything. The first couple of months were spent cleaning and training new staff, and then the orders started arriving.

As those initial orders came through, Anna said Paul and Jean Mooty and sometimes even a couple of Jean's friends worked with the other employees to prepare the shipments. Whatever it took for the mill to rise again. Paul wrote in an e-mail to me, "There is not one thing [Jean] has not done here from washing windows, cleaning bathrooms, painting, running retail, counting inventory, planning tent [now warehouse] sales and the anniversary event. This has been a true family venture and there is nothing we would not do."

On September 15, 2011, the mill celebrated its reopening with Governor Mark Dayton, other officials and guests. Father Erik Lundgren gave the blessing, and Mayor John Jasinski read a proclamation, declaring the day as Faribault Woolen Mill Day.

The Mootys were chosen as the *Faribault Daily News* Citizen of the Year in 2012. A black plaque engraved in gold states, "In recognition and honor of your leadership and for your undying efforts to make Faribault a better place to live." Also in 2012, the Faribault Woolen Mill Company was awarded "Best of MN" for the "Best Reborn Minnesota Brand." In 2013, the Southeast Minnesota Sheep Producers Association (SEMSPA) presented the Faribault Woolen Mills with a plaque that states, "For your Continuous Support and Promotion of the Sheep Industry."

In June 2012, the *Faribault Daily News* announced that Chuck would be the interim CEO of Fairview Health Services. Yet he remained the CEO of the mill because "the company has a big chunk of the business it needs right now to stay busy, the brand and operations are on track, and cousin Paul Mooty, the woolen mill's CFO, will be on hand to oversee day-to-day operations." Chuck eventually became the CEO of Jostens, leaving the mill position to Tom Irvine in October 2013; Irvine stayed with the business until January 2015.

In 2014, water again concealed the dam. This time, however, the mill was sandbagged and saved. On our tour, when the photographer, Jillian, and I stood in the deepest, dampest part of the mill, Paul pointed to a glass-block window and then showed us a video on his phone of a fish swimming in it, a reminder of Louis Schwichtenberg's pickerel story from the 1936 flood.

My youngest brother lunched with a high school friend in Colorado in the summer of 2015. He mentioned to her that I was writing a book about the mill. His friend Mary exclaimed she had a Faribault Woolen Mill blanket in her car. She had bought it at a vintage store when she went to a wedding near Minneapolis two summers before. "I had always wanted a wool blanket," she wrote me, "to keep in the car (picnics! warmth/safety!), and I loved the pattern."

Faribault Woolen Mill Company blankets: recognized and adored everywhere.

THE LAWSUIT

According to public documents available at the United States District Court Clerk's Office, District of Minnesota located in Minneapolis, a civil action was filed on December 19, 2012: *Hilda L. Solis, Secretary of Labor, United States Department of Labor v. Michael Paul Harris, the former CEO, President, and Chairman of the Board of Directors of the Faribault Woolen Mill Company.* The secretary of labor is later listed as Thomas E. Perez. The extensive collection of documents includes correspondence, motions and sworn statements.

On June 23, 2015, the three-day bench trial began. The opening statement was made by Ruben Chapa on behalf of the secretary of labor: "The matter presented today is an action brought by the Secretary of Labor against Defendant, Michael P. Harris, for violations of the Employee Retirement Income Security Act [ERISA] for failing to remit employee contributions to the Faribault Mill's health plan."

Further:

> *As the evidence will show, Defendant Harris breached his fiduciary responsibilities with respect to the Faribault Mill's health plan. The underlying promise of ERISA pursuant to Section 404 (A)(1)(a) is that ERISA fiduciaries have an unqualified obligation to forward the plan assets without regard to their own conflicting interest. The facts of this case are fairly simple, Your Honor. Defendant Harris and the Faribault Mill's finances were intertwined. Therefore, when Defendant Harris could raise no more money, either from his own means or through external sources, it resulted in the failure to meet his own debt obligations and those of Faribault Mills. One of those debts was the employees who had their employee contributions withheld by Faribault Mills for remittance to the health plan's insurance provider, HealthPartners. Defendant Harris used Faribault Mills' monies to fund lavish trips around the world several times a year, charged his children's college education directly to company credit cards, placing it on his expense report.*

The facts show the direct nexus between Defendant Harris and Faribault Mills was that he also had his relatives lend Faribault Mills' money and he himself mortgaged his home to keep Faribault Mills afloat. The witness testimony and documentary evidence will show that Defendant Harris was a fiduciary of the health plan from at least January 1ˢᵗ, 2009, through March 27ᵗʰ, 2009. As fiduciary, he breached his fiduciary obligations pursuant to Section 404 (A)(1)(a) of ERISA, which requires that he act for the exclusive benefit of the participants and beneficiaries.

Lincoln Loehrke, counsel to Harris, made the following opening statement:

This is what the evidence will show. Mr. Harris was not personally involved in any decision not to remit the health plan employee contributions. To the extent Mr. Harris took any affirmation actions regarding the health plan, those actions involved rubberstamping the plan selection made by Mr. [__], the VP of human resources, and signing plan insurance checks presented to him by Ms. [__], the CFO. Neither of these actions are the actions subject to Complaint in this litigation.

Mr. Harris did not exercise authority or control to cause Faribault Mills to not remit health plan employee contributions. Likewise, Mr. Harris did not cause the plan to engage in any transaction, much less a transaction in which he knew or should have known constituted a transfer or use of plan assets for the benefit of a party in interest. Mr. Harris also did not self-deal, and he did not act disloyally with respect to the plan.

At one time, Mr. Harris was the CFO, President, and Chairman of the Board for Faribault Mills. Faribault Mills was a complex business with multi-state operations, dozens of employees, and two different plants and a retail store, a full complement of corporate officers, and an independent Board of Directors.

Faribault Mills operated in a difficult industry and had been struggling for years. It was the last vertically-integrated Woolen Mill in the entire country. It was about to close in the late 1990s when Mr. Harris and others invested in the company and saved it. Mr. Harris returned in 2001 when Faribault Mills was again struggling and facing closure. At that time, Mr. Harris reengaged with the company and successfully raised the capital needed to save it a second time.

This is when he took on management responsibilities at Faribault. Mr. Harris also owned a miniscule portion of the company stock, 0.3 percent, and had Common Stock options which he never exercised. Mr.

Harris' key contributions to Faribault were sales and capital. He traveled extensively to raise funds for the company and successfully secured financing and sales from international sources. Under Mr. Harris' leadership, Faribault Mills became a premier blanket manufacturer with substantial orders from the U.S. Government, large retailers like Target, Wal-Mart, and Bloomingdales, and numerous hospitality companies, both domestic and international. Nevertheless, the profitability in this highly challenging industry was elusive.

And then the financial crisis struck. In 2008, raw material costs exploded. Customers no longer paid on time. Financing dried up, and cash flow became a problem, not only at Faribault but throughout the industry. Mr. Harris responded to these financial challenges in a manner which can only be called extraordinary and which we all should applaud. When his CFO, [___], notified him that the company lacked funds to pay all expenses, Mr. Harris filled the gap with his own money. He loaned the company approximately $1 million. Mr. Harris was not a man who had $1 million laying in his bank account somewhere. To raise those funds, he mortgaged his family's home, cashed in his retirement, and put up essentially every dollar in his name.

The judge has not yet returned a decision as of this printing.

Chapter 9

ONE OF THE LAST MILLS
IN AMERICA

As a citizen of Faribault who has lived here for over thirteen years, I ask myself: how important is it that the Faribault Woolen Mill Company has reopened? It's really a ludicrous question if you ask employees, others who live in town and Faribault Woolen Mill aficionados. Faribault is not just about sandstone cave blue cheese and Bishop Whipple. "In the last half of the twentieth century," a video from the company stated, "the mill was creating over half of the wool blankets made in America." In small-town Faribault. Now the reinvented yet traditional, well-known and cherished mill in southeast Minnesota is out to impress even more.

"If this were Chuck and Paul's blanket company," Paul Mooty told me, "no one would care."

Faribault Woolen Mill goods are sold at more than five hundred boutique retailers, such as Crate & Barrel, West Elm, Restoration Hardware, JCrew and Anthropologie. Just as in the past, department stores like Bloomingdale's carry the woolen mill products. The mill's goods are also featured in five showrooms across the country. Products appear in catalogue retailers such as the Sundance catalogue, Land of Nod and Guideboat.

Magazine ads since the reopening have appeared in *Martha Stewart*, *GQ Magazine*, *Vogue*, *Esquire*, *Architectural Digest*, *Redbook*, *LDB Interior Textiles*, *Lonny Magazine*, *Gear Patrol*, *Apartment Therapy* and *Collective Quarterly*.

Around the nation, 130 undisclosed corporations, including Fortune 500 companies, give blankets as business or hospitality gifts. The Hudson in New

York and the Sundance Resort in Utah are two of the hotels that feature Faribault Woolen Mill goods.

Partnerships have included JCPenney, Target, Caribou Coffee and Duluth Pack. Actor, director and screenwriter George Clooney bought everyone on the set of *The Monuments Men* a monogrammed military-type blanket. The mill made personalized blankets in 2014 for each of the thirty-two NFL teams as Minneapolis bid for and won the hosting of the Super Bowl in 2018. The mill introduced over one hundred new products to celebrate its 150th anniversary.

"Most important of all," Bruce Bildsten, partner and chief marketing officer (CMO), wrote in an e-mail, "every product we make has our name proudly on the label, even for luxury brands like Ralph Lauren and Rag & Bone."

The billboard on I-35? It changed. It now has a woman wearing a wool scarf, lounging on a black-and-white plaid blanket with another person. It reflects the updated retail name, "The Mill Store," as well as the business's current navy logo. The bottom has easy four-step directions to the store.

The directions came in handy when the mill hosted its annual September sale. Up until 2015, it was under a tent; in 2015, the ads claimed the mill had outgrown the tent, and the sale was held in one of the mill's warehouses. If it were a concert, it would have been a sellout. Droves flock to this event because of the special deals on high-quality woolen items. When Jillian and I toured the plant with Paul and he showed us "seconds" (the products with imperfections), we just shrugged. We saw nothing amiss. It must be the same for customers who are looking for that label, the one that says Faribault, because it means comfort and it means quality, sometimes at a bargain price.

If anyone asks Paul about production numbers and profits, he'll tell you that as a private company, he doesn't want those numbers divulged. If they've been published in the past, they didn't come from him. He wrote in an e-mail to me, "To know that at one time this mill produced over one half of the blankets sold in the U.S. and was a nationally recognized brand tells you that this mill has capacity and ability to produce a meaningful volume of goods."

He explained further: "Just like a house, you need to build a good foundation, and that is what we are doing."

The current management team includes Paul; Bruce; Terry Mackenthun, partner and CEO; and John Leholm, vice-president of finance. Though the actual number fluctuates depending on the season and orders, approximately one hundred employees currently produce the mill's goods.

In a newspaper article two years after Paul and Chuck bought the mill, Paul said, "I have to give credit to the former employees who came back

The 2015 Faribault Woolen Mill management team: John Leholm, Terry Mackenthun, Paul Mooty and Bruce Bildsten. *Photo by Jillian Raye Photography.*

to work for us. They are the reason we have been able to accomplish what we have."

Jake David related several stories of his first forty years and then second three years at the mill after it reopened. He spoke of working with Dick and Bob Klemer and Elmer Schultz, all of whom, he said, were "very good to me."

When Jake turned seventy-nine in the fall of 2014, he had a cake at the mill, shared with his wife, who had her birthday the day before his. Jake praised Paul for not only taking his wife on a tour when she admitted she had never been on one but also for giving the couple two blankets. Jake said, "This was special. Really special. It shows they appreciate you. And I appreciate it, too, for what they've done. They didn't have to do it."

THE MILL STORE

Go back to the beginning. Go back to the store.

The retail store was started by Paul Mooty's wife, Jean, when the mill reopened. Its first day of full-time business was May 15, 2012. When the mill opened its doors in 2011, the store was more sideshow than anything, open only a few hours a week. A pop-up store in Mall of America during November and December 2011 helped revive the mill's relationships with its customers and spoke to the holiday masses that the mill was back. This led to the remodeling, to the reopening, to the rebirth of a brand practically everyone thought had disappeared forever.

On an early summer day, I was researching the history of the mill in its archives in a bank vault on one side of the store. I overheard a man say, "It's a beautiful day to show my friend Faribault, Minnesota." I left the mill's packed archives and asked where the man's friend was from.

"Houston, Texas."

We introduced ourselves, and Father Erik Lundgren and I shook hands. Father Erik told his story: he grew up in Edina, where Chuck and Paul also grew up. His family had the orange mill blanket in the back of their Volkswagen. Here, he had been assigned to the Catholic church, Divine Mercy, but had moved to the Twin Cities area for his next assignment. He still felt compelled to return to Faribault to show off the mill to his friend. Father Erik told me that he takes some credit for the mill reopening. He said he moved to Faribault during the flood in 2010, and every time he'd take his daily run, he prayed to Mary to let the mill reopen. When the Mootys bought it, he asked if he could say a blessing at the grand opening. He was invited to do so, sprinkled holy water and said his blessing. We said goodbye, and Father Erik and his friend continued to look around the store.

Later that afternoon, a woman from New York and a man from Chicago stopped in the mill store. Visitors from New Mexico also came in to look at the Faribault Woolen Mill Company's goods.

Jana Woodside, the store manager who also gives the tours, was talking to a customer about the history of the mill as she rang up purchases, answering questions about the mill's reopening. She spoke of the Mooty cousins and told the customer that "they are intelligent businessmen but with huge hearts."

"Wow," the customer replied. "It really makes you want to work for them."

This makes me think of other comments. Anna said, "The Mootys care more about family. They care about their employees." Tom Klemer said that the Mootys "were the type of owners I was looking for…the Mootys are, from all I've heard and seen, good stewards of the mill, and I'm happy that they came in when they did."

Jean Mooty said, "The mill gets in your blood."

THE FARIBAULT WOOLEN MILL COMPANY TOUR

The eleven o'clock tour is full. Jana begins by telling the group of a dozen—from pre-teens to a senior citizen—a short history of the mill. She speaks of Carl Klemer with Jenny on her carding treadmill, how the mill had to move to the current location after the third fire, of the leads from the departments who were asked back in 2011 to not only continue the mill's deep traditions but also to train a new generation of workers.

Now, Jana continues, New York and California are the biggest markets outside Minnesota. Everything from small boutiques to department stores like Nordstrom have carried Faribault Woolen Mill products. Jana also speaks of hospitality consumers, such as the Waldorf Astoria hotel, one of the first buyers after the reopening. The Windstar cruise line has the mill's blankets on deck chairs; West Point cadets receive blankets from the mill.

Most of the domestically sourced wool the mill uses comes from farms in Montana and Idaho; the super-fine merino wool used for premium projects is imported from New Zealand and Australia. The mill no longer scours its wool, however; this is done in Texas or South Carolina. Scouring the wool

The scour machine in the basement of the mill was damaged in the 2010 flood. *Faribault Woolen Mill Archives.*

The flood of 2014 made the Cannon River dam nearest the mill disappear. Employees and community members sandbagged the mill. *Photo by Audrey Kletscher Helbling.*

is the dirtiest job, one that removes mud and manure, one the mill used to do with a machine in the basement, but it was damaged in the 2010 flood and needs repair. When the Cannon River rose again in 2014, community members and employees helped sandbag the area, preventing the water from again flooding the basement.

Jana tells the story of how the equipment was within weeks of being shipped to Pakistan when the Mootys bought the mill. Leads of departments were personally called by the Mootys or visited in person. After apologies for what happened when it closed, the Mootys asked the leads to come back and train the new workers; others came back when they heard the news. Before the tour group follows Jana through the store and into the mill, she mentions we'll probably see Mary Boudreau, the employee who has worked at the mill for almost sixty-one years.

Once inside the mill, Jana tells us that taking photographs is allowed, except of the new release hanging on the burling machine. We walk along the path marked by two painted white lines. Jana explains that the mill's products go through approximately twenty-two steps before they're ready for customers.

The first photo opportunity is of the empty green bin that will soon have hundreds of pounds of scoured wool, weighed for its fiber content. The non-digital scale looks decades old but still works with precision. This

LOOMED IN THE LAND OF LAKES

Above: A veteran employee stock dyes wool, an artisan process used for decades. *Photo by Jillian Raye Photography.*

Right: This process of measuring dye is still used today. *Faribault Woolen Mill Archives.*

weighed wool goes into a picking machine that rakes out large clumps. This equipment is also used in blending fibers. For instance, portions of dyed black wool and natural white will be weighed and blended. As fibers blend in manufacturing, they'll offset one another to create a heather gray. Colored wool is also used to weave multicolored designs, such as plaids and patterns. Next is the hopper that gives the fiber buoyancy and sucks out debris.

Jana explains the dye process, which mostly takes place in the basement where the tour does not go. Loose fiber is "stock dyed." This means sizeable amounts of wool are dyed in large vats after the fiber is washed. The employee in charge of dyeing has been with the company about forty years. On the first floor near the washers, he also "piece dyes," when the fiber is already woven into a blanket or throw.

To the left of the painted path is a recycling machine. Anything from raw wool to woven fabric can be thrown in and mixed up to be reused. From the mill's point of view, this not only provides a lower price point for particular products but also produces less waste.

Once the wool—still considered "raw"—has gone through the hopper, it is sent to one of the nine carding machines, each machine actually like a set of twins. As the tour group enters a massive warehouse-looking area, my jaw drops, the space more immense and loud than I imagined. Jana's voice must compete over the deafening sound of the machines. The first machine cards the wool into batting, the thick sheet used for quilts. This batting is folded over itself in narrow sheets, looking almost like dense ribbons of icing. A bridge then takes the batting up and over the heads of the employees and sends it to the second machine. This carding machine with its rollers and combs blends the fibers and aligns them to go in the same direction. The strands that come off the carding machine are called roving, loosely twisted and easy to pull apart. Jana gives everyone a piece of the roving to feel for themselves.

Jana leads the tour group to the spinning frames next. Employees thread the roving through small rollers. The strands are slightly stretched and twisted onto spinning bobbins, which are below the rolls of roving. Jana gives us a sample of yarn to feel, a strand of wool much stronger now that cannot be pulled apart.

The next piece of equipment, the coning machine, performs the opposite task—a single strand of yarn from a bobbin below fills a cone above, which is about half as tall but twice as thick as a bobbin. Three bobbins fill a cone. Employees constantly perform quality tests to ensure the machines keep doing their jobs.

This close-up of a carding machine shows part of the intricate rollers, combs and chains vital to the carding process. *Photo by Jillian Raye Photography.*

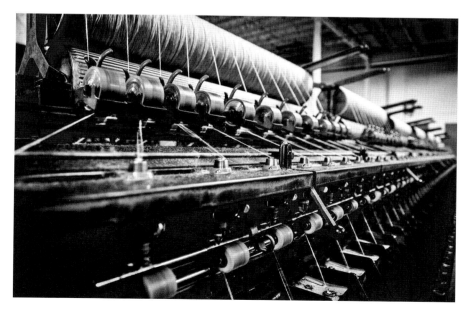

One of the frame spinner machines in the mill. The roving is on top. *Photo by Jillian Raye Photography.*

This coner machine is the next step for the yarn after spinning. The cones are on top. *Photo by Jillian Raye Photography.*

Still shouting over the decibels of the machines, Jana leads the group to the weave shop, which is actually in the same immense space as the carding, spinning and coning machines. As Jana starts explaining the warper, a woman next to me—who later explains she has an engineering background and is fascinated with manufacturing—leans close and voices in my ear, "This is what America used to look like." I understand what she means. This mill is filled with skilled, hands-on workers—artisans—taking raw material and sending it through several steps to become a fine finished product.

The tour group stands at the end of the warper, which almost resembles a spider web or a time travel machine when seen from the end. Metal frames called creels approximately fifty feet long line up like fences on either side of a path, each side with six rows of numbered pins that hang specific colored cones. The yarn from the cones travels to a ten-foot-long warp beam at the end, like a giant's spool of thread, and wraps around the beam.

Probably one of the words most associated with weaving is loom. One type of loom is the dobby loom, used for ninety-degree angles. A warp beam is placed at the end of the loom. The yarn on the warp travels lengthwise through the loom. The fill or weft yarn is threaded through the warp yarn on

These long strands of yarn come from cones hung on metal creels that lead to the warper beam. *Photo by Jillian Raye Photography.*

a shuttle as it crosses the yarn back and forth. Patterns on dobby looms are programmed in and read like a punch card or self-playing piano. The yarn on a warp beam will make between 300 and 350 blankets. The jacquard looms are for the designs and patterns. These looms are controlled by yellow harness cords that reach nearly as high as the ceiling. The harness cords look like a yellow waterfall spilling from the ceiling but hum like bees. These cords control about two thousand needles. Jana points out that one loom cutting fabric in half is making robes, or smaller blankets.

From across the area, Jana points out Mary Boudreau, working away at one of the looms. Jana says that Mary is always surprised at the attention she gets for having worked for six decades at the mill. "Mary," Jana says, "likes to tell a good story." Mary is always interviewed for newspaper articles and news features, but she believes, it seems, that she is just doing her job. Jana waves at Mary from across the weave shop, and Mary waves back.

The tour group walks out of the machine-laden space, and Jana's voice goes back to soft spoken. At the peak of manufacturing, she explains, 175 people worked three shifts in order to make blankets during the world wars. I point out the typewriter-looking machine on our right, and Jana explains that this is what programs the older looms. The plastic cylinders

This blanket with a map of St. Paul is about to be inspected in the burling shop. *Photo by Jillian Raye Photography.*

Finding imperfections and trimming edges is still an essential part of the mill's product process. *Faribault Woolen Mill Archives.*

Fringe is found on some of the mill's blankets and other goods. *Photo by Jillian Raye Photography.*

with punched-out circles are what guide the looms. Only one individual regularly programs this machine.

The next stop on the tour is the burling shop. After hanging on a metal frame, blankets or throws slide up and across an illuminated diagonal surface where employees check for imperfections in the weave and trim up the sides. Heavy blankets go through this process twice. If a product's imperfection is glaring, Jana explains, it may be reground and recycled. Otherwise, it may be sold in the mill store as a factory second. Most often, customers don't even notice the imperfection.

After a product goes through the burling process, fringe may be added. Ends are cut with a six-inch gap. The ends are twisted, and thread holds the twist in place. A hot wash with agitation secures the thread.

As the tour group moves past piles of finished goods, Jana explains that the softness of the products depends on the kind of wool. It is inevitable that several people on the tour touch the samples to feel for themselves. Jana then leads the group to the wash house, where the goods are washed and shrunk. The washer was bought after the mill reopened. Ultimately, the length of the wash depends on the softness of the blanket or throw. One thousand pounds of fabric can be washed in a day.

One of the newer washing machines that washes and shrinks all the woven fabric. *Photo by Jillian Raye Photography.*

This wash house is the room with the windows above the dam cascade, where if you look from the other side of the Cannon River, ghosts of white words from the 1920s appear on the brick face from when this room was on stilts. Today the windows are open, as they must be almost every day, to help quell the humid indoor air. Step to one window; ducks swim dangerously close to the dam, the lake reaches to the left, Father Slevin Park on the right leads to the other dam and the Rice County Fairgrounds' full parking lot announces another event there. Mary's nephew is the employee who washes the fabric and tells me that this room, where these windows lend such a fine view, is the best spot in the mill to work.

The veteran dye employee also piece dyes on a large machine near the washroom where the view is. His son also works for the woolen mill.

Once the fabric is washed, it moves to the two-story dryer. Wet, folded fabric leaves a rectangular metal tub on one end of the room and is lifted up and through a joint that drapes the fabric like a thick clothesline high above the floor. Machinery pulls it flat as it mimics the burling motions, up and over and across. Pins guide the fabric; if the hot water shrunk it too much, the pins can pull it back out. The dryer also applies detergent for the washable woolens.

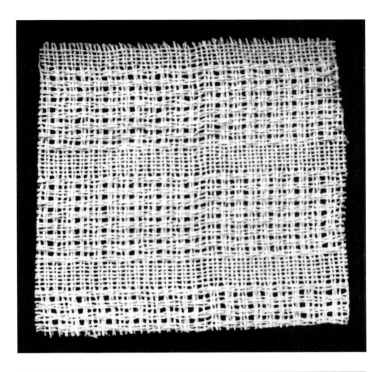

The photo on top is of woven fabric; the photo on the bottom is of napped fabric. *Faribault Woolen Mill Archives.*

Sewers add the final touches to the Faribault Woolen Mill's products. *Faribault Woolen Mill Archives.*

The last step on the first floor is napping. Napping gives loft to the fabric and increases the warmth. As Jana explains, it's like "a cloud over a body of fabric."

Upstairs on the third floor, an area unseen by tour groups, employees check for quality a final time. Goods are cut, edges are sown and labels are attached. Once the products are carefully packaged, they're usually brought

Each woolen product, such as these coffee cup sleeves, is given the same quality care. *Photo by Jillian Raye Photography.*

down on carts in the elevator to be stored on the second floor until shipped. Each woolen averages the twenty-two-step manufacturing process in up to six weeks. Currently, the mill has one shift from 6:00 a.m. to 2:30 p.m. on weekdays to produce the products.

The mill has attempted to cross train some of its employees, so that others can take time off for vacations or family affairs. Someone in the tour group asks Jana about her family connection.

"The mill was dinnertime talk," Jana says, as her dad, Alan Woodside, was the vice-president of sales for almost ten years after beginning his mill career in the sales department. Yet another example of the mill's decades-long framework of family.

The conversation circles back to the Mootys. "The Mootys had everything we needed," Jana says, "including timing."

The best step they took, Jana says, was nominating the mill for the National Register of Historic Places. Because of this designation, a grant and tax credits helped pay for renovations to keep Minnesota's oldest manufacturer in business.

Jana ends the tour by saying that today a lot of mill traffic is from out of town. When it first reopened, local residents frequented the mill. They never assumed it would actually be gone and had maybe even taken it for granted. The mill has been well received ever since the reopening. The Mootys stepped in, and the rest is, of course, history.

THE KLEMERS NOW

I visited Tom Klemer, Carl's great-great-grandson, at his Edward Jones office in Faribault. I had a lot of questions for him about his family, the mill and what happened when the last Klemer president, his dad, left.

At one point during our conversation, I asked if he would ever consider going back to work at the mill. After a pause, he replied:

I don't know. There's been times where…I don't know if I would or not. My heart and soul is still in that building. I used to go with my dad when I was a kid, he'd go into work on Saturdays…It was me and Dad and nobody else—that was my mantra every week, me and Dad, nobody else. So my dad and I would go to work, and I had this big, dark playground of all these departments and piles of wool and creepy warehouses that I was exploring, creating my own little playground. That was awesome and very dear to me. That's why, you know, when you ask if I'd ever go back…I know it wouldn't be the same, but it's…it would be interesting. I don't know. And, plus, part of it is, you know, I've…lost a lot there. And it would be hard that way and going in in a different role. So I don't know, it would have to be the right thing and the right opportunity and obviously some security because I've reinvented myself a few too many times in my life, much to my wife's chagrin.

Tom's brother Dave lives in a town nearby, and a sister lives "Up North" (Minnesota); the other sibling lives in Alaska. Though Dave has stepchildren and has been a foster parent, Tom is the only one of the four who has children. Tom's oldest two had once expressed interest in the mill, but the daughter just left Faribault for a new job in the Twin Cities. The oldest son?

"Right now, he's working for a guy that refurbishes organs and tunes organs, church organs, in Morristown," Tom said. "Actually, he's pretty good with carpentry, so my wife's encouraging him to be a cabinetmaker."

My eyes opened wide. A cabinetmaker just like Carl.

"Another full circle," I said.

The youngest son is interested in becoming an Edward Jones agent like his dad, and Tom's wife also works for the company. In 2015, Tom's youngest daughter gave birth to Carl Klemer's great-great-great-granddaughter, the seventh generation. Time will tell if she finds her way to Minnesota, not by ox cart but by car or plane, to the Faribault Woolen Mill Company that stands strong on the banks of the Cannon River.

THE 150ᵀᴴ ANNIVERSARY
CELEBRATION

On a Minnesota Saturday in August, so hot and humid that the cloudless sky stretched gray, the Faribault Woolen Mill Company hosted its 150th anniversary celebration near the mill and at Father Slevin Park, the lawnscape between the two dams. It was time to celebrate success.

Soon would be the first-ever running of the sheep. Flexible orange plastic fences ran on either side of a runway maybe fifty feet long; inside was a single white post ten inches off the grass, extended from side to side. People were leaving the other part of the celebration to file across the narrow dam pedestrian bridge to see the spectacle.

A friend came near, wanting to share the shade of a tree. I asked her why she was attending the 150th anniversary. She said that she liked to support the local people and local festivals.

"The mill has been here a long time," she continued. "This is a big deal."

She paused and watched the growing number of onlookers lining both sides of the run, pointing out a few she recognized.

Bruce Bildsten escorted Mary Boudreau as she got a head start between the orange fences, walked over the pole and headed to the finish line. My friend next to me said, "Isn't it lucky the Mootys bought the place? Otherwise, it would've been standing vacant…the mill is actually great for the whole state."

In decades, the mill went from fire to sky to failure to triumph.

The emcee announced the people running with the sheep, including employees and guests, about ten in all. When the gate of the trailer opened,

The first-ever running of the sheep during the mill's 150th anniversary. *Photo by author.*

People leave the running of the sheep and cross the dam to attend the 150th anniversary festivities. *Photo by author.*

the sheep pushed their way to the back of the trailer instead of out of it, their fright apparent. The owner of the sheep prodded them out from the back, and one sheep fell out of the trailer. A lemming move, all the sheep then darted out of the trailer and ran with the people. It was over in less than a minute. Later, Paul Mooty said, "That was fun. I think that might have to become an annual event."

Back at Slevin Park, the vendors included the Minnesota Lamb and Wool Products and the Textile Center. At the latter, people practiced some of the art the mill does daily, such as carding and weaving. The Hasse family from nearby Pemberton brought its petting zoo with sheep, goats, rabbits and a lot of miniatures: donkeys, ponies and a llama. The place was full of children taking their chances to pet the animals, sanitizing their skin afterward when their parents finally pulled them away.

Mixed among food trucks with cheesecake, brats, ice cream and BBQ were local favorites: Basher's Backyard Cabin, Lyon's Meats and the Cheese Cave. Many savored the new F-Town Brewing Company's beer. Face painting, a beanbag toss and a traveling photo booth in a VW bus called Blue Goose shared the park space. The local Kona Ice truck sat by itself across the river near the mill building, inviting those with sweat rivulets coursing down their backs to visit the tents over on that side, too.

Paul invited people to gather by the large stage for a short program. First, he thanked those who came. Then he spoke of four years earlier when he and his cousin Chuck bought the mill. Paul said, "While it certainly has been a lot of hard work, it has been a deeply rewarding and humbling experience and something that has had a great sense of 'it was meant to be.'"

He introduced Father Erik Lundgren, the one who had prayed that the mill, locked and gathering dust, would reopen as he ran by it each day when he lived in town. "Father Erik's prayers were answered," said Paul.

Father Erik first shared that his parents had owned a Faribault Woolen Mill blanket in their family's VW bus, joked that it could very well be one of the reasons for his existence. Then he shifted to serious for prayer. Father Erik thanked God for "creative spirit" and for "giving gifts." He thanked the Klemer and Johnson families. He then asked the crowd to reach out their hands toward the mill, and he led the blessing, reminiscent of a similar gesture when the mill celebrated its grand opening in 2011, asking the mill to stay open to provide for those who needed warmth and those who needed work for the next 150 years. A grand opening. A celebration. Far removed from its closing years before.

Paul returned to the podium:

While today is a celebration of the mill's 150th anniversary, we want to remember why we are here: we are here because of all of those who came before us with their innovation, leadership, dedication and commitment, and we are also here because of the employees who returned to the mill in 2011 to make the revival of this mill possible—some of those employees with twenty, thirty, forty and even fifty or more years of service to the mill at that time. I can tell you, without question, we would not be here today without them.

I know how proud the Faribault community is of the mill, and I know how proud each and every one of us who works for the mill is as well. Today is a time to celebrate a storied past and to look forward to the next 150 years.

Paul then introduced the guests and dignitaries: U.S. senator Amy Klobuchar; Faribault mayor John Jasinski; former Minneapolis mayor R.T. Rybak; Nathalia Faribault, great-great-granddaughter of Alexander Faribault; Tom Klemer, great-great-grandson of Carl Klemer; and Pete Johnson, grandson of Ed Johnson. He also asked the mill employees past and present to raise their hands and be recognized.

"The history of the mill was built by these great people," Paul said, and the crowd applauded. Paul also recognized those who couldn't be at the celebration, namely his dad, Melvin, and Chuck's dad, John, who had taught their sons the importance of hard work and deep family values.

Paul also thanked Jocelyn Okubo, a friend of his who volunteered to make a one-of-a-kind blanket from scraps, the image of the 150th anniversary, as well as the mill's logo. This blanket hung on the bridge that crossed from Slevin Park to the mill parking lot, occasionally blowing in the breeze, a slight tear here and there from the pull of Mother Nature.

Once introduced by Paul, Senator Klobuchar thanked the crowd and former Faribault mayor Chuck Ackman. About the mill's closing, she said, "The story didn't end. The workers had a dream that dreams can be pulled from the wreckage." She spoke of Dennis Melchert, who kept going to the mill when it closed to check that the equipment still worked. She spoke of the "broader story of manufacturing in America," how the mill makes "wholly made" products. She said, "It is a story of daring; a leap of faith; believing in purpose, product and people; a story of resilience."

Back at the podium, Paul told the audience:

Today will mark the beginning of the Faribault Woolen Mill Hall of Fame, and we will be inducting seven noteworthy individuals. Over 150

The 2015 Faribault Woolen Mill employees on the bank of the Cannon River in front of the iconic mill. *Photo by Jillian Raye Photography.*

years there are obviously many, many people who deserve to be recognized and it is our intention, on an annual basis, to induct additional members to the Faribault Woolen Mill Hall of Fame and share their stories and contributions to this great mill.

Today, our first seven members represent the first six presidents of the mill from the Klemer and Johnson families, whose leadership and stewardship built this mill into what it is today. The seventh person is a current employee, who in 1954 at the age of eighteen began her career here at the mill and continues with us today as she approaches sixty-one years of service.

Chuck Mooty, after telling the crowd Paul had forgotten to thank himself, honored Carl Klemer; Faribault mayor Jasinski honored Ferdinand Klemer; Bruce Bildsten spoke of Frank Klemer; Nathalia Faribault introduced Robert Klemer; Tom Klemer honored his dad, Richard Klemer; and Terry Mackenthun introduced Pete Johnson. Finally, Paul honored and congratulated Mary Boudreau, who stood beside him.

Before the program ended, Bruce explained that his son had a response to the mill "wanting to do something charitable." The mill marketing team asked thirteen Target designers to create something out of mill scraps. A silent auction of the items would raise money for Habitat for Humanity. Products ranged from sauna hats to stuffed sheep, a sleeping bag to a suspended teepee, a braided rug to a reversible hooded poncho. Bids easily reached and then jumped into three figures with only a few people on each auction sheet.

Bruce also mentioned the Memory Mill, a new digital experience that the mill hopes will last for generations:

> *Faribault blankets have a history of becoming heirlooms, wrapped in stories and memories of the past. We designed the Memory Mill to give blanket owners the ability to create memories for the future—thoughts and intentions that will stay with their blanket or throw as they pass it on to its next owner.*

The mill now makes metal labels with their own unique number IDs to register at memorymill.faribaultmill.com. They can be sewed onto woolen products to ensure that a "memory thread" corresponds to the product. The hope is that these threads will be preserved forever in order to "pass on traditions and memories."

It was then the mayor's turn to give his proclamation to end the program. On September 15, 2011, when the mill reopened, the mayor said the slogan for the day would be "beans, blankets and blue cheese." Now with the new F-Town Brewery, he said for August 15, 2015, the new slogan would be, "Welcome to Faribault, the town of beans, blankets, blue cheese and beer." The mayor then read the proclamation, in it hoping that the legacy of the Klemer and Johnson families would continue.

Under a long tent, people watched a short movie about the mill. Narrated by Mary Boudreau, it highlighted the mill's beginnings and accomplishments, the Klemers and the Johnsons, making blankets for the military. Words on the screen told of its being empty for eighteen months, that the equipment was tagged for Pakistan. Mary said:

> *At the last minute, Chuck and Paul Mooty stepped in and saved it for us. Family ownership again. They're investing in new equipment and hiring more people. They reopened the mill in 2011 and brought back many of the old workers. They focused on what made this mill great: pure wool blankets and throws. Then we started making scarves for the first time. The time was right. People cared about things made in America. They were ready to invest in quality. Our woolens are made to last for generations and can be handed down. This mill will be around for another 150 years. I believe it.*

Just behind me was a young woman with a little boy on her lap. When Mary appeared on the screen, I heard her ask the boy, "Who is that? Is that great-grandma?" Later I found him playing in the grass, and I asked him if he'll work for the mill someday, too, follow family tradition. He looked down, too shy to speak.

"Maybe he'll be the president," the young woman answered for Mary's great-grandson. "He can run the whole company."

Indeed.

BIBLIOGRAPHY

Atwater, Isaac. *History of the City of Minneapolis, Minnesota, Part II*. Albany, NY: Munsell, 1893, 657. books.google.com/books?id=0cZg4L4sbBwC&dq=hilliard+who+started+theminneapolis+woolen+mill&source=gbs_navlinks_s.

Bildsten, Bruce. "The Faribault Woolen Mill Story." vimeo.com/86042147.

Binkley, Mike. "Finding Minnesota: Faribault Woolen Mill: Providing Warmth Since 1800s." WCCO, November 2, 2014. minnesota.cbslocal.com/2014/11/02/finding-minnesota-faribault-woolen-mill-providing-warmth-since-1800s.

Brown, Curt. "Minnesota History: Tilt-A-Whirl Gives Faribault, Minn., a Historic Spin." *Minneapolis Star Tribune*, April 2, 2015.

Butler, Corey, Jr. "Shaken, but Not Broken: Faribault Mills CEO Says Company Will Stay the Course." *Faribault Daily News*, March 7, 2009. www.southernminn.com/faribault_daily_news/archives/article_8e939401-7435-5f0b-99db-689dec36053f.html.

Cartwright, R.L. "Duluth Ship Canal Opening, 1871." MNopedia. Minnesota Historical Society. Last modified May 2, 2015. www.mnopedia.org/event/duluth-ship-canal-opening-1871.

The Cathedral of Our Merciful Saviour. "History of the Cathedral." www.thecathedralfaribault.com/index.php?p=1_9_A-Brief-History.

City of Faribault, Minnesota. "Historic Preservation." www.faribault.org/316/Historic-Preservation.

CNN. "70 Historic Moments from the 1970s." August 17, 2015. www.cnn.com/2015/05/21/world/gallery/70-historic-moments-from-the-1970s.

Commercial West. "Faribo Blankets Blanket the World: On Firm's 100 Anniversary." May 22, 1965, 20–22.

Davey, Katie Jean (reference librarian). "U.S. Dakota War of 1862: Overview." Gale Family Library, Minnesota History Center. libguides.mnhs.org/war1862.

BIBLIOGRAPHY

Factory Guide. Faribault Woolen Mill Co. 1865. Pamphlet.

Faribault Daily News. "City Welcomed Flour Mill in 1862." April 3, 2011. www.southernminn.com/faribault_daily_news/archives/article_9a05d315-c86d-5a09-b203-c6c94b5c1d7c.html.

————. "Reusing Woolen Mill Store Is Smart." December 14, 2009. www.southernminn.com/faribault_daily_news/archives/article_29df3996-8f92-53ee-b71f-b834d800ab01.html.

Fate, Kay. "Woolen Mill Future Remains Unclear." *Faribault Daily News,* July 15, 2009.

Feyder, Susan. "Weaving a New Business Plan: Cousins, and Experienced Businessmen, Paul and Chuck Mooty Have Big Plans to Resurrect the Beloved Faribault Woolen Mills." *Minneapolis Star Tribune,* July 25, 2011.

"Flammable Fabrics Act and Product Safety Commission Hearings Before the Subcommittee on Commerce and Finance of the Committee on Interstate and Foreign Commerce: House of Representatives, Ninetieth Congress." April and July 1967. Washington, D.C.: U.S. Government Printing Office, 1967. www.stewartlaw.com/Content/Documents/HR%20-%20Flammable%20Fabrics%20Act%20and%20Product%20Safety%20Commission.pdf.

Fossum, Paul R. "Early Milling in the Cannon River Valley." *Minnesota History* 11, no. 3 (1930): 271–92. Minnesota Historical Society Collection. collections.mnhs.org/MNHistoryMagazine/articles/11/v11i03p271-282.pdf.

Frey, Martha. "Historic American Engineering Record: North Star Woolen Mill." Historic American Engineering Record. Omaha, NE. May 1998. lcweb2.loc.gov/master/pnp/habshaer/mn/mn0500/mn0559/data/mn0559data.pdf.

Gales, Elizabeth. Faribault Woolen Mill Company National Register of Historic Places Registration Form. National Park Service, United States Department of the Interior. December 30, 2011. www.mnhs.org/shpo/nrhp/docs_pdfs/0024_faribaultwoolenmill.pdf.

Granger, Susan. "Faribault's Historic Contexts: Final Report of a Historic Preservation Planning Project," 23–25. [Gales, Elizabeth. National Register of Historic Places Registration Form, December 30, 2011.]

Helbling, Audrey Kletscher. "Historic Faribault Woolen Mill Opens Retail Store with an Artsy Vibe." Minnesota Prairie Roots blog. June 12, 2012. mnprairieroots.com/?s=faribault+woolen+mill+store.

Hogsett, Don. "Faribault Parent Taps Masko." *Home Textiles Today* 21, no. 30 (2000).

"How to Revive a Mill." [unreadable] *Express,* November 1, 1954. Faribault Woolen Mill Archives.

Jarvis, Jeffrey. *Book of Memories,* 2011. www.cannonvalleymills.com/wp-content/uploads/2011/09/woolen-mill-memory-book.pdf.

Klemer, Frank H. "History of Faribault Woolen Mills: 1865–1940." Presented to the Rice County Historical Society, Faribault, Minnesota. October 22, 1940. *Faribault Daily News,* October 24–25, 1940.

Klemer, Robert W. "Addendum I to History of Faribault Woolen Mills: For the Years 1940–1960." Unpublished.

————. "Addendum II, History of Faribault Woolen Mills: For the Years 1940–1960." Unpublished.

Lindberg, Joseph. "Faribault City Council Forgives Woolen Mill Assessment." *Faribault Daily News*, June 29, 2011. www.southernminn.com/faribault_daily_news/archives/article_78639d44-065a-578b-9ae8-27f5ad674057.html.

———. "Faribault HPC Investigating Historic Signage for Woolen Mill." *Faribault Daily News*, July 23, 2012. www.southernminn.com/faribault_daily_news/news/article_a6b91462-0975-5e1b-8a15-c52efaf2eebe.html.

———. "Faribault Woolen Mill Now on National Register of Historic Places." *Faribault Daily News*, June 27, 2012. www.southernminn.com/faribault_daily_news/news/article_5224441a-d905-5608-a758-3f6e8a3b3f08.html.

———. "History Renewed: The City Is Helping the Faribault Woolen Mill in Its Effort to Secure a Spot on the National Register of Historic Places." *Faribault Daily News*, March 15, 2012.

Lira, Carl. "Biography of James Watt." Michigan State University College of Engineering. Updated May 21, 2013. www.egr.msu.edu/~lira/supp/steam/wattbio.html#dates.

Minneapolis Journal. "New Incorporations." December 28, 1905, 4.

Minneapolis Tribune. "Minneapolis: The Head of Mississippi Navigation and the Manufacturing and Railroad Centre of the North West." January 7, 1868. [Gales, Elizabeth. National Register of Historic Places Registration Form, December 30, 2011.]

Minnesota Historical Society. "Building History." Mill City Museum. www.millcitymuseum.org/building-history.

Mittelhauser, Mark. "Employment Trends in Textiles and Apparel, 1973–2005." *Monthly Labor Review* (August 1997): 24–35.

National Down Syndrome Society. "What Is Down Syndrome?" www.ndss.org/Down-Syndrome/What-Is-Down-Syndrome.

Peterson, Susan E. "Faribault Woolen Mills to Merge with Blanket Maker Dakotah: Companies Will Keep Their Names." *Minneapolis Star Tribune*, September 9, 1998.

———. "Group Buys Majority of Faribault Woolen: Investors Plan Mill Expansion." *Minneapolis Star Tribune*, April 29, 1998.

Powell, Joy. "A Long History—and Now, a Future; Founded Near the End of the Civil War, Faribault Mills Is the Oldest Private Company in Minnesota—but It Hasn't Made Money in 13 Years. Now a Contract to Make Blankets using a Corn-Based Fiber from Cargill Dow Has Put the Firm on the Cutting Edge." *Minneapolis Star Tribune*, October 30, 2003.

Rodenborg, Rebecca. "Faribault Woolen Mill Co-Owner Reflects on First Two Years." *Faribault Daily News*, July 25, 2013. www.southernminn.com/faribault_daily_news/news/article_c9c55f36-a457-55aa-b59b-9f8e4be7054c.html?mode=print.

Roorda, Allison. "Woolen Mills Closing Affects Colorado Mill." *Faribault Daily News*, March 22, 2011.

Rubin, Cynthia Elyce. "Faribault Woolen Mills: Tradition & Change." *Fiberarts* 26, no. 5 (March/April 2000): 10.

Schreiber, Pauline. "Faribault Residents Have the Chance to Discuss the Removal of Two Dams." *Faribault Daily News*, August 14, 2003. www.southernminn.

BIBLIOGRAPHY

com/faribault_daily_news/archives/article_deac0f65-a7c7-54c2-a397-13a5112c7750.html.

———. "'Largest Blanket' to Be Built Saturday for Heritage Days." *Faribault Daily News*, June 22, 1990.

Shinola Detroit. "Introducing the Shinola Supply Blanket by Faribault Woolen Mill." September 17, 2014. www.shinola.com/journal/introducing-shinola-supply-blanket-faribault-woolen-mill?___store=en_us.

Smith, Jaci. "Faribault Woolen Mill CEO Takes on New Role." *Faribault Daily News*, June 1, 2012. www.southernminn.com/faribault_daily_news/news/article_ac6f4527-f583-5083-bd39-0cbfc25adb4a.html.

Southernminn.com. "Faribault Woolen Mill Opening." Video, 2015. www.southernminn.com/youtube_67ec2f32-cb66-51a4-852b-e2f59b7b8716.html.

———. "Faribault Woolen Mill Store." Video, 2015. www.southernminn.com/youtube_be395f10-0174-5a5a-9031-66bfe57c1f45.html.

Thomas E. Perez v. Michael Paul Harris, 0:12-cv-03136-SRN-FLN (United States District Court, District of Minnesota, St. Paul Division). [Originally *Hilda L. Solis v. Michael Paul Harris*, 0:12-cv-03136-SRN-FLN. Filed December 19, 2012.]

Vomhof, John, Jr. "Minnesota's Super Bowl Bid Included Faribault Woolen Mill Blankets." *Minneapolis/St. Paul Business Journal*, May 21, 2014. www.bizjournals.com/twincities/blog/sports-business/2014/05/minnesota-super-bowl-faribault-woolen-mill-bid.html.

Ware, Brenda. "Remembering the Woolen Mill." *Faribault Daily News*, December 22, 2010. www.southernminn.com/faribault_daily_news/archives/article_b87c51e6-2936-530e-98d5-5bd0055f477a.html.

Wee, Heesun. "'Crazy' Innovative: How One Entrepreneur Is Reviving 'Made in America' Wool." CNBC, March 12, 2014. www.cnbc.com/2014/03/12/from-sheared-sheep-to-finished-recreating-the-made-in-usa-wool-supply-chain.html.

INDEX

ABOUT THE AUTHOR

Lisa M. Bolt Simons is a writer and educator who has lived in Faribault for over a decade with her husband and boy/girl twins. She earned her bachelor of arts from Drake University, her master of education from the University of Minnesota–Twin Cities and her master of fine arts from Minnesota State University–Mankato. She has received grants, awards and finalist or honorable mentions for both her nonfiction and fiction. Find out more at www.lisamboltsimons.com.

Photo by Jillian Raye Photography.